INVESTOR RELATIONS

INVESTOR RELATIONS

Neil Ryder
AND
Michael Regester

Hutchinson
Business
Books

Copyright © Neil Ryder and Michael Regester

The right of Neil Ryder and Michael Regester
to be identified as authors of this work
has been asserted by them in accordance
with the Copyright, Designs and Patents Act 1988

First published in Great Britain by
Hutchinson Business Books Limited
An imprint of Century Hutchinson Limited
20 Vauxhall Bridge Road, London SW1V 2SA

Century Hutchinson Australia (Pty) Limited
20 Alfred Street, Milsons Point, Sydney
New South Wales 2061, Australia

Century Hutchinson New Zealand Limited
PO Box 40–086, 32–34 View Road, Glenfield,
Auckland 10, New Zealand

Century Hutchinson South Africa (Pty) Limited
PO Box 337, Bergvlei 2012, South Africa

British Library Cataloguing in Publication Data
Regester, Michael
 Investor relations.
 1. Great Britain. Public companies. Communications with
 shareholders
 I. Title   II.   Ryder, Neil
 658.4′5′0941

ISBN 0–09–173959–4

Phototypeset by Input Typesetting Ltd, London
Printed and bound in Great Britain by
Butler & Tanner Ltd, Frome and London

To
the ever-supportive
Christines

. . . and all the other long-suffering spouses
who put up with absent, distracted or
distraught partners for the sake of industry

Acknowledgments

We particularly wish to express our appreciation to the following people for the invaluable help they provided in compiling this book: Alexandra Hockenhull, for research; Clyde Walton, for consistent good advice and guidance; all those who helped check facts and figures, in particular David Bentata, Claire Horton and I R Japan; and Caroline Searle and Cheryl Cooley for their endless patience in typing and retyping the manuscript.

Neil Ryder
Michael Regester

CONTENTS

————PART IV————

IS IT ALL WORTH IT?

Preface

For ten years I was fortunate enough to earn a living as a journalist. While scribbling for a newspaper is not an occupation universally admired or respected, at least friends and family knew what one did between the hours of nine (well, eleven at the latest) and five. Since becoming involved in investor relations, I have developed the keenest sympathy for demographers, systems architects and life scientists. We are all pioneers struggling against impossible odds to explain to people what we do for a living.

Investor relations is a young and immature industry even in the United States. In Britain it is in its infancy. Long recognized – to the extent that it has been recognized at all – as a minor branch of public relations, or a week-end pursuit for industrious finance directors, investor relations is finally coming to be seen as one of the most central and time-consuming functions of senior corporate management. The reasons are not hard to find.

A company's equity is its most valuable currency. The price at which it trades will help to determine the cost of capital for growth and acquisition; the strength of the company's defence against unwelcome suitors; and the wealth of the institutions and individuals that own the currency. As Neil Ryder and Michael Regester continually underline, the purpose of investor relations is not to secure the highest possible share price, but the optimal price which most fairly reflects the actual prospects of the company. In placing more emphasis on investor relations, the UK corporate sector is at last recognizing shareholders for what they are – the owners of British business.

For many companies, this axiom is strangely unfamiliar. The graveyard of UK plc is littered with tombstones bearing the legend 'I ignored my shareholders' or, more often, 'I remembered them too late'. When I was writing the Lex Column on the *Financial Times* some years ago, I passed on to the chairman of a large and grand British company dissatisfied comments that I understood had been made to him by several of his leading institutional shareholders. He replied with some pride that this was quite impossible as he made a point never to speak to his institutional shareholders, or at least never to the young and arrogant fund managers with whom I had no doubt been gossiping. Whether it was young and ignorant shareholders or quite another variety who three months later prised the chairman from his office, a year before the company was taken over, I never found out.

But equity is not only a transaction currency to be used by or against incumbent management. It is also a resource, ranking alongside a company's products, brand names and fixed assets. A consumer branded goods company will invest enormous amounts of time, energy and money in researching the market for its product. It will understand the profile of its buyers, know its distributors, and track its competitors. It will be the life-blood of the business.

But, until recently, the corporate sector has devoted hardly any effort to understanding and satisfying the customers of that other resource, its equity. The retailers of the product in the broking houses and the consumers in the investing institutions have been viewed with the distant suspicion that British industry has always reserved for the City – overpaid, overbred and over there. Relations between the City and industry are probably no closer now than before. If anything, the upheaval caused by Big Bang has heightened the corporate sector's concern about the quality and integrity of financial advice.

But there is undoubtedly a greater recognition on the part of the corporate sector that it needs to establish stronger and more regular relations with financial audiences and, above all, with the key investing institutions. As it enters its tenth consecutive year of rising profits, the corporate sector is robust, affluent and self-confident. It has come to value good relations with its owners and has recognized that developing those relations is a job which should be undertaken by the senior management of the business as well as by spokesmen, stockbrokers and advisors. The best investor relations advice that can be given to the boards of British business is – do it and do it yourselves.

Michael Regester and Neil Ryder have set themselves the daunting challenge of mapping out the contours of a continually changing landscape. Like early cartographers, they found that developments and discoveries in the field changed the shape of their subject even as they were writing. So, as they are the first to admit, *Investor Relations* cannot be a definitive text. But what they have produced is the first comprehensive delineation and description of the territory of investor relations in Britain. And that is no small achievement.

John Makinson, Makinson Cowell investor relations consultancy.

PART I

PREPARING THE PROGRAMME

CHAPTER 1

What's it all about?
– the purpose of investor relations

'Judging by the way relationships between companies and institutional shareholders are deteriorating . . . attempts to break the mould may not be too far away.' (Barry Riley, *Financial Times*, 20 May 1989.)

'This is an Italian operation on the Italian market and that is the context. If the shareholders want it they can take it and if they don't they can leave it.' (Raul Gardini, chairman of the Feruzzi group, responding to criticism of his controversial plan to restructure the Ferruzzi-Montedison group, *Financial Times*, 24 December, 1988.)

These two quotes illustrate the two extremes of opinion on shareholder communication, and they go to the heart of the current controversy about investor relations (from now on we will refer to this as IR) – should investors be expected to take a passive role in the companies they part own, voting with their feet if they feel their interests are being ignored or should they be expected to take an active interest in the company's affairs?

Assessing the problem – or opportunity

In the USA – where 92 per cent of the companies for which a takeover bid was made in 1988 actually lost their independent public status (41 per cent to a 'White Knight') – the Financial Relations Board estimates that expenditure by the 10,000 actively traded public companies on IR grew from $4 billion in 1983 to $5.4 billion in 1988.

In the UK, there have been 34 contested bids (greater than £75 million) since the October 1987 crash. Only six of the target companies remained independent. No-one measures IR expenditure, but interest in the discipline has soared and head-hunters report enormous difficulty in finding people with useful experience.

In France, where the president of the EEC Commission expects to see 10,000 French companies alone involved in cross-border mergers by 1992, the Bourse has made it mandatory for every company to designate a 'spokesperson' on IR matters. Germany and Japan have recently been shocked by hostile bids for large companies – most unusual in these two countries, where banks dominate the ownership of most large companies.

Even in Switzerland, that stronghold of cosy capitalism, the market is changing irrevocably, with two large companies already allowing foreigners to own registered shares (though not yet to have equal voting rights).

The global securities market is finally coming of age (see Chapter 7) and, while that does not make globetrotting IR necessary for every company, it does mean ever-increasing competition for funds and attention – even in domestic markets – with the 25,000 companies listed on the world's top 20 stock exchanges.

As if this was not enough, the willingness of the bankers to finance highly-leveraged takeovers, and structural changes in most of the major markets – particularly in the European Community – are leaving most companies at least bemused, if not dangerously out of touch, and possibly vulnerable.

Who does a chief executive report to?

The chief executive's primary role is to run the company, and to ensure that it performs as well as can be expected in the prevailing circumstances. He may well feel – as Raul Gardini apparently does – that, as long as this is done, the shareholders should leave him to get on with it. We can all think of other CEOs who appear to feel the same way – 'Tiny' Rowland, Carlo de Benedetti, Robert Maxwell *et al.* (Incidently, references to chief executives and other roles in this book are all in the masculine gender for reasons of simplicity and ease of reading only.)

The boards of Guinness, Next, Habitat/Mothercare and many other companies around the world seemed to be shocked, though, when disappointed shareholders exacted their retribution. But how many CEOs would tolerate superficial, uninformative or unintelligible executives – even the most successful ones? And if they did ignore such arrogance for a time, what would they do if it eventually became clear that the culprit had actually been hiding a performance much less successful than had been assumed? Why are they surprised when the owners of the company behave as they would have?

How many finance directors insist on highly detailed and carefully verified reports from the company's hard-pressed operators and then produce reports to the shareholders that obscure the true position? What do they expect if the truth emerges?

Your responsibility?

Many chief executives and other directors of publicly-owned companies accept that it is their responsibility to keep the owners informed. Some only do so because they perceive a threat and feel the need to win their shareholders' loyalty. Some have recognized that changes in the financial community have made it impossible to rely on the company's broker, banker or other advisers to do it for them – just as they discovered the danger of letting employee communication become dominated by union officials. Some have recently taken up their positions and have always believed in the power of communication. Some even recognize the very positive, strategic role that IR can play in their company.

But these enlightened executives may feel a need to understand more about what IR involves, what it could do for them, and what part they should play in it personally.

This book cannot hope to cover the whole ground – IR in the USA would require a book in its own right – but, at the very least, we hope to give an overview that will be helpful, and thought-provoking.

Hype or hypothesis – what is IR?

IR has been variously described as the most necessary, superficial, overdue, controversial, valuable, time-consuming, under-exploited discipline in management today. Its critics claim that it is nothing but a defensive or aggressive attempt to 'hype' the company's shares. Its practitioners and other proponents argue that they spend as much time limiting expectations as they spend raising them, and that there is more to it than simply trying to manage the share price.

That is not to say the share price is unimportant. After all, you may need to issue shares to raise cash for expansion, or to pay for an acquisition. If neither, and the company's focus is on improving its existing business, you could become the target for someone who can use you to increase his company's earnings per share simply because his shares are rated more highly than yours – like JWT and the 'mini-conglomerates' did. Or you could fall prey to someone with more global ambitions – like Rowntree did. If none of these apply, the chances are that investors will become so bored that the share price will drop to the point where you become attractive simply as an asset or tax play – like Dunlop or Consolidated Goldfields.

It is, therefore, distinctly in the company's interest to attain, and retain, the highest share price that is consistent with an accurate and informed view of the company's performance and its realistic potential. The cynics have it wrong, because any company that encourages the share price to go beyond this optimal level is courting disaster (ask Acorn!) – the disappointment that will inevitably occur will destroy, possibly permanently, the trust in the management team.

Meeting the demand

So, the share price does matter, and it is hard to think of another area of a company's business where demand dictates price but in which the average company makes so little effort to manage the demand in a professional manner.

One notable exception is our friend Warren E Buffet, chairman of Berkshire Hathaway Inc – a legend in his own time for growing his company's share price at a compound rate of 23 per cent during his 23 years in the position so far, as well as for his witty, honest, informative and readable chairman's statements. We gain the following insights from his February 1989 statement:

'Our goal is to attract long-term owners who, at the time of purchase, have no timetable or price target for sale but plan instead to stay with us indefinitely. We don't understand the CEO who wants lots of stock activity, for that can be achieved only if many of his owners are constantly exiting. At what other organization – school, club, church, etc – do leaders cheer when members leave?

'. . . Of course, some owners will need or want to sell from time to time, and we wish for good replacements who will pay them a fair price. Therefore we try, through our policies, performance and communications to attract new shareholders who understand our operations, share our time horizons, and measure us as we measure ourselves.

'If we can continue to attract this sort of shareholder – and, just as important, can continue to be uninteresting to those with short-term or unrealistic expectations – our shares should consistently sell at prices reasonably related to business value.'

After 23 years of 23 per cent compound growth, Warren E Buffet can afford to be relaxed about his company's share price and the demand for its shares. Yet he still expresses strong views on both and we will return to his comments throughout the book.

But Mr Buffet makes a strong point about the expectations and time horizons of investors. Clearly, if the company is investing heavily in long-term projects with considerable potential, it is foolish either to allow its share price only to reflect its depressed short-term prospects or to fail to make any effort to attract investors with long-term horizons.

Matching liability and return

'We needed to develop a detailed picture of who they [the share-holders] were and mount an effective communications programme to sustain their commitment during the difficult times ahead.' (John A Griffiths, finance director, BET, writing in *The Treasurer*, May 1989.)

As we point out in Chapter 3, some investors have short-term liabilities (eg, investment/unit trusts) and some have regular or long-term liabilities (eg, most pension funds and insurance companies). It behoves the company to match its needs with those of its investors, which can take considerable research, planning and effort. There is little point in a drug company with no new drugs on the market but several very promising drugs in the expensive development phase, seeking short-term investors. On the other hand, a computer company with a temporary product lead may want high turnover in its shares to push the price up, if it needs to raise cash for a big production and marketing launch.

In 1987 the CBI city-industry task force heard the usual winges about short-termism on the one side and the familiar grumbles about inadequate information and contact on the other. But it concluded that companies need to sell themselves harder to the financial community.

The good old days

We hear regular cacophonies of complaint about short-termism from managers in the USA and UK – and increasingly now in Europe. Yet there are ample examples of companies which have successfully retained their shareholders' loyalty, and hence their independence, throughout long product development cycles or profound downturns in their markets – if they have explained these issues clearly.

As pension fund managers frequently point out, it is often company pension managers and trustees that demand – and replace their fund managers as a result of – quarterly performance statistics.

At one time, a company could rely on its house broker to act as its intermediary with investors, but house brokers are no longer in a position to fulfil this responsibility because their protected world has fallen apart around them in the UK and is currently doing so through-out Europe.

One or two jobbers used to handle all trades in a particular share, so they knew all about the market for those shares. But markets are fragmenting all over the world, with security houses consolidating on an international basis and seeking transaction fees rather than relying on continuing relationships to cover their ever-increasing costs (imagine the howls of protest if an industrial company's head office displayed the gross extravagance now common amongst securities houses, banks and insurance companies; most of us could fit our entire offices inside the average bank's tree-filled lobby!).

Europe more unified

'The financial markets in the European time zone will be more open and more unified than those in either Japan or the USA.' (The Right Honorable Sir Leon Brittan, QC, vice president of the EC Commission, 18 May 1989.)

In both the USA and Europe, deregulation has irrevocably changed the scene. The abolition of exchange controls in the UK in 1979 was probably the most important step yet in changing the market. Almost immediately, 20 per cent of UK-managed funds moved into foreign equities. UK companies could no longer rely on a captive pool of investment capital and their passive – or non-existent – shareholder relations became inadequate. Two thirds of the EC countries will be following the same route by June 1990.

Discussion has started on unified monetary policy in Europe and – probably more important and inevitable – moves are afoot to create a unified stock market, at least for the bigger companies in Europe. European companies will have to learn to live with an increasingly international market for their shares. As we point out in Chapters 7 and 10, EC and international regulations are playing an ever-greater role in investment and financial markets and in company affairs.

Differences in accounting policies make international comparisons difficult, but intensifying competition between fund management groups makes foreign investment essential to beat the global indices. Companies need to come to grips with the complex information needs of these international investors – both in terms of content and com-munication.

One good example is the proposal by the UK Accounting Standards Committee which aims to bring UK companies into line with international standards on the treatment of goodwill. This, if it sticks any better than their proposals on current cost accounting, would require UK companies to include goodwill on acquisitions on their balance sheets and amortize it against profits. This could significantly reduce their profits, although it would give a huge boost to the balance sheets of acquisitive companies. According to its US accounts, for example, BET would add almost £1 billion to its assets, but it would have to charge at least £25 million against its profits, although it would obviously be able to restate former years to show the same (or a greater) growth rate.

On the other hand, these complex problems bring with them the enormous opportunity for companies to increase their funding flexibility, tapping markets all over the world and possibly cutting their cost of capital as well as their dependence on domestic investors.

Securitization

'$102 billion of US equity was taken out of the market in 1988 through share buy-backs and leveraged buyouts alone.' (Salomon Brothers, 1988 Global Equity Markets.)

Companies also have to adjust to the trend towards 'securitization of debt' – the issue of paper to raise debt capital instead of equity. This blurs the distinction between debt and equity; brings in new kinds of investors; makes credit ratings necessary; makes the debt market completely global; and the types of information required by creditors are different from those of equity investors.

This too, then, complicates the company's IR obligations while creating opportunities. But a parallel trend might have more immediate impact: the increasing fashion for leveraged bids – using debt as well as equity to pay for the acquisition – changes the valuation of companies from being based primarily on earnings, dividends and assets to relying more on cashflow and interest cover. Vulnerability, strength and value change accordingly, and so does the IR picture.

Sharing a Porsche

'Notwithstanding the existence of Chinese walls, conflicts will arise.' (Fred Vinton, NM Rothschild & Sons, *The Treasurer*, March 1989.)

Following the abolition of exchange controls, the Thatcher Government pushed the UK financial community into another major series of changes – Big Bang. This, followed by the crash in October 1987, caused a complete restructuring of the UK market – much of it following what had happened in the USA and what is starting to happen in other European markets.

The brokers, who had been industry's main conduit to the City, lost much of their credibility as conglomeration and then competition aroused fears of conflict of interest, greed and worse. So having lost the jobbers with their total knowledge of the market for their shares, companies lost their chief means of communicating with their investors.

Fund managers, likewise, lost much of their main source of information. They still trust some of the brokers, but they are becoming increasingly public in their condemnation of most. In New York, the same trend led to a massive growth in 'buy side' analysis (funds hiring their own research analysts) and some of the UK funds have started to move in the same direction. A bloodbath in the UK brokers' research departments is widely expected and companies are therefore likely to have to cope with considerable growth in the number of buy-side requests for meetings.

Concentrated control

'For some years, we have been concerned by the increasing power of the investing institutions, the narrowing of the market place which this implies, and the volatility which a high level of institutional ownership brings to equities.' (Brian Basham, chairman, Broad Street Group, 13 March 1989.)

Naturally enough, fund managers have reacted to the changes by seeking more direct contact with, and communication from, companies. But whereas the CEO or finance director could maintain a close relationship with a dozen analysts or so, he cannot hope to keep up with even the top ten per cent of fund managers, never mind their subordinates and all of the tens of thousands of smaller funds.

Even if he could, there isn't time for the research and planning required to ensure that the people important to you get priority, or for the constant day-to-day questions which arise.

The question of who should share the load with the CEO is dealt with in Chapter 2, but we *are* talking about *sharing* the load – there is no question of the CEO or finance director avoiding it altogether. In particular, he will have to be involved with setting the objectives and policies and with meetings with at least the key fund managers.

Big Bang, international competition and other structural changes in the market have hastened the trend towards concentration in ownership in the UK equity market, just as similar changes have in other markets. Individual ownership of UK shares has been steadily falling for years, from nearly 60 per cent 25 years ago to probably less than 20 per cent last year – the actual number is hard to calculate because some individual owners hold their shares through nominee accounts.

The institutions, therefore, probably own three quarters of all the shares. And a relatively small proportion of them own an increasing percentage of that holding. Furthermore, investment management is being concentrated in ever fewer hands, as more and more funds are handing over the job to specialist management firms.

Index linking is also concentrating control, since a fund which links its investment to the index is essentially handing control to those same active managers.

The same trend is running in the USA, where institutions currently own about 35 per cent of equities but are expected to reach 50 per cent by the year 2000. They already account for 80 per cent of the equity trading on the New York Stock Exchange (which is the favourite amongst individual investors, so the percentage is probably higher on the other exchanges) and they are becoming more active in what Americans call 'corporate governance' issues.

Interference or investor protection?

'Ministers must now be nasty. They should threaten the cartels with the wrath of Sir Gordon Borrie. They should remind the institutions that they hold their tax privileges on sufferance. They should warn them not to assume the arrogance of owners when they are no more then stewards.' ('City Comment', *Daily Telegraph*, 8 February 1989.)

In Europe, direct shareholder activism is not unheard of, but it is unusual. However, the UK has its own breed of collective activism, through the Investor Protection Committees (IPCs) of the main institutional associations – the most active of which are the National Association of Pensions Funds and the Association of British Investors.

It is a peculiar reflection of the faith placed in the probity of British financial institutions that the system allows these bodies not only to impose their own guidelines on UK companies but also to vet proposed moves by companies in advance. Thus, some companies discuss highly price-sensitive plans with representatives of the very bodies best placed to profit from such information. Unaccountably – given the scandals which have shaken the City – the justification given is that the IPC members impose strict Chinese walls between themselves and their colleagues!

Yet, despite the strict and cumbersome investor protection measures laid down in new laws by a government supposedly committed to the encouragement of wider share ownership, this most extraordinary IR practice is allowed to continue.

Furthermore, this same government has yet to change the rules which prevent public companies from selling new shares to the public. Companies have been encouraged – or even driven – to use their shares to acquire businesses much bigger than themselves, despite the disasters this has sometimes caused, by institutions hungry to generate froth in the market, and by bankers seeking huge fees. Yet, the IPCs have been allowed to impose draconian restrictions on the sale of new shares to anyone other than the existing owners. Given that many of the individuals cannot afford to take up their rights to such issues, this means that the large institutions not only receive their entitlement, but they also receive a portion of the remainder – since they have usually underwritten the issue (guaranteed to take up any rejected portion) – as well as the underwriting fees.

The IPCs argue that their insistence on these pre-emption rights is a protection for small shareholders, but logic and history suggest that it might be more a matter of self-interest – a surviving element of the pre-Big Bang cosy cartels that ran the City. Some companies argue that it is unwarranted interference with their ability to raise money at competitive rates – which would surely be good for all shareholders (the loss of underwriting benefits only affects some).

Reactionary or revisionist

'[The Stock Exchange] is under intense pressure as large securities houses develop their own support services, which they are making commercially available.' (John Moore, Assistant City Editor, *The Independent*, 11 May 1989.)

What inflames most company directors is not having to argue their case with large shareholders (they are entitled to self-interested views and most responsible directors welcome the useful interchange of views) but the massive degree of control the institutions can exert as cartels.

Another example of collective monopoly in the UK, which many are beginning to resent, is the Stock Exchange itself. Having restructured itself when forced by the OFT to do so, the SE nevertheless remains under the control of the large City firms. With overheads higher than the much bigger New York Stock Exchange, it has helped the rise in costs to a level which may have forced its members to compromise some of their ideals. One example has been the changes allowing a delay in reporting of large transactions, which has reduced companies' ability to follow the market in their securities.

An even more controversial issue as far as IR goes is the creation of the TAURUS system for processing share transactions.

The exchange has been torn between conflicting demands amongst its owners – those same securities houses – to the extent that, at the time of writing, it is not clear what TAURUS will be able to do.

The plan is to 'dematerialize' shareholdings (ie, do away with share certificates as legal proof of ownership), which worries those who want to encourage individual ownership since it is not clear that private investors will approve.

More seriously, TAURUS is intended to become the system which records every transaction and it is not clear how much detail it will make accessible. A company cannot communicate effectively with its shareholders if it cannot identify them. The existing system has been difficult to live with, although the more advanced companies have evolved sophisticated systems which track their owners fairly effectively. The creation of TAURUS will not only make five-day rolling settlement possible – a big advance on two-week fixed 'accounts' – but could provide almost instantaneous and much more detailed 'transparency' of transactions.

Yet it is not clear that the SE will take up this opportunity fully – and the reason goes back to its failure to try to understand companies' IR needs in the early stages of the TAURUS discussion, and to the issue of collective monopoly. One of the noticeable contrasts between the exchanges in London and New York is that the latter tends to treat its listed companies as important customers, whereas the former tends to treat companies like troublesome schoolboys who need to be caned occasionally and should otherwise be seen (though only through its screens) and not heard.

No wonder companies and government officials have started to question whether the SE should be allowed to retain its monopoly over trading shares! Systems like Reuters', together with company registrars, companies themselves or some of the security houses, would be perfectly capable of setting up alternative dealing systems to compete with the SE and it is beginning to look like a mistake that this issue was not considered earlier.

Alternatively, ownership and control of the SE could be changed; no-one has asked whether the funds using the system and the companies abused by it would be prepared to pay towards the cost of the ideal TAURUS system.

The changes taking place in the methods of trading and recording share ownership are of deep concern to many listed companies, and companies need to keep up with these changes and express their views forcibly.

Wider dissemination of information

'A company must ensure that all shareholders are provided with equivalent information.' (The Right Honourable Sir Norman Lamont, QC.)

Likewise, responsible IR executives question the Stock Exchange's monopoly for receiving company announcements. Under pressure from the Office of Fair Trading, the Investor Relations Society and others, the Exchange decided to launch a 'regulatory news service' which would give equal access to company news to other information providers as well as to its own TOPIC service. It is allowing itself plenty of time to prepare for competition and, during the delay, the major institutions who can afford to subscribe to TOPIC will continue to receive this price sensitive news before other investors – hardly a system which meets the spirit of UK or EC regulations, or the apparent ideals of the Government. Even when the new system is introduced, and Reuters or other information services are finally allowed to compete with TOPIC on equal terms, one can still question whether it is appropriate for a body with monopoly trading rights and regulatory responsibilities to be involved at all with an organization which makes profits from supplying sensitive information. In the USA, competing exchanges receive pre-notification of announcements to enable them to regulate their markets, but the news is given to investors through separate channels. In the UK, suitable channels exist, but perhaps the absence of competing exchanges has caused a more complacent attitude.

Indeed, UK companies, too, are at fault – very few make any effort to time their announcements to suit their domestic – let alone foreign – investors. The trend has been towards early morning announcements, which guarantees that large institutions enjoy several hours trading before most private investors see media reports and whilst US and Japanese exchanges are closed. Perhaps we have ourselves largely to blame for the decline in private share ownership!

Wider share ownership

'As companies grow more frustrated with their institutional shareholders, they are tempted to sell themselves directly to the public.' (Barry Riley, *Financial Times*, 20 May 1989.)

Given the restrictive nature of the UK's institutional investment cartels, then, it is small wonder that most ambitious companies yearn for wider share ownership and are prepared to put more time, effort and money into IR programmes aimed at achieving it.

Many have started seeking foreign shareholders for other good reasons. They recognize that the globalization of the market will either turn them into international equities or leave them in domestic backwaters. They are determined to achieve the lowest cost of capital and the most flexible funding. They see the commercial advantages of a local profile wherever they do business – and the benefits in terms of employee involvement. But these objectives also fit well with a general wish to reduce the proportion of domestic control to a manageable level, where institutions are recognized as vital, often far-sighted, and loyal investors – no more than that.

However, there is another – often easier – means of achieving broader ownership: to increase the proportion of shareholdings amongst domestic private investors. This is not currently an easy task, but more and more large companies have seen the success of Sid and other successful marketing programmes by the Government. These have helped to push the number of private shareholders up from three to nine million in the last few years.

These dramatic moves have not yet created a stable system of 'popular capitalism' – it is estimated that 56 per cent of UK private investors own shares in only one company. Yet they held remarkably steady in the 1987 crash and the Government seems determined to continue to push towards this ideal.

Stockbrokers have signally failed to help; marketing direct to the public would have been expensive and would have required management and marketing skills which they had failed to develop. So they have largely retreated and left it to unit trusts and the like to invest the public's savings – despite signs that the public increasingly resists such 'institutionalization'. The banks and building societies, too, have been reluctant to develop this market.

The Government, despite its public pronouncements, appears confused. By creating Personal Equity Plans (PEPs), it has encouraged yet another form of institutionalized savings, and most PEP managers charge high fees to the investor who insists on choosing his own investments (if they allow it at all). Business Enterprise Schemes also gained tax advantages but, laudable though the aim may have been, they have done little for real companies and have largely siphoned off the savings of 'high net worth' individuals into schemes designed principally for tax efficiency.

As yet undaunted, a number of large companies have started co-operative studies into the feasibility of marketing their shares direct to the public – and possibly even providing a dealing service to small investors.

Many companies have had very satisfying experiences with employee share option schemes. In this area, IR effort can also bring employee motivation and loyalty benefits, and make a direct contribution to the bottom line.

The Government has now given a (slightly half-hearted) tax boost to employee share ownership plans (ESOPS) and many boards are studying the potential here too. However, the complexities are daunting and the Government has not yet succeeded in persuading the IPCs to exempt these from their restrictive guidelines.

But, as a lot of companies provide dealing facilities on their share option schemes and either administer or pay for the administration of these schemes themselves, it may be worth their while to extend similar facilities to other individuals. Once again, the Government has not, so far, given much encouragement by lifting the restrictions in the Companies Act.

It may be that the UK will see the emergence of efficient, well-marketed, low-cost equity dealing businesses but, failing that, it begins to look as if companies will have to rely on their own efforts to manage their shareholder bases more actively and more professionally.

In search of excellence

'In special cases, due to the calibre and personality of the IR officer, I speak to him more than the CEO and allow him to influence my perception of the company'. (UK Trust Manager, quoted in Equity International/Taylor Nelson survey, February 1989.)

We shall discuss the tactical challenges and benefits of IR to:

- reduce the overall cost, and increase the flexibility of the company's funding
- identify and broaden the company's shareholder base
- defend against takeover
- assist in the identification and execution of acquisitions
- improve commercial visibility and employee motivation.

It would, however, be wrong to neglect its strategic importance. By creating closer links with investors, it can help the company to ensure that it develops strategies which will be welcomed by the owners, rather than meeting expensive and humiliating defeat.

At the heart of the role is the maintenance of adequate demand for the company's securities at a price which accurately reflects its true potential amongst investors whose investment horizons and policies match those of the company.

The planning and execution of this role will, like the marketing of the company's products, require substantial discipline, co-operation and effort.

If the IR programme sets out to provide the information on which investors can judge the company's potential, those responsible for it will be walking on a knife-edge. If some of the information they give is not price-sensitive, it is of no value to the investor; if they give such information out unevenly they create insiders who cannot legally trade in their shares.

Their most valuable assets are credibility and trust; if they once lose these, they become useless to their company – and possibly to any other.

The IR role, therefore, requires professionalism, tact, honesty and sensitivity. These are encouraged by the regulatory bodies, the practitioners in the market, and by the Investor Relations Society – which exists to promote higher standards of IR and which, by providing a forum for the exchange of best practice, and a representative voice for all listed companies, has done a great deal to help the directors of public companies to fulfil their obligations to their owners.

CHAPTER 2

Who's holding the short straw?
– allocating the responsibility

To the shareholders of Berkshire Hathaway Inc.:

'Our gain in net worth during 1988 was $569 million, or 20 per cent. Over the last 24 years (that is since present management took over), our per-share book value has grown from $19.46 to $2,974.52, or at a rate of 23 per cent compounded annually.

'Two years ago I told you that we needed profits of $3.9 billion to achieve a 15 per cent annual return over the decade then ahead. Today, for the next decade, a 15 per cent return demands profits of $10.3 billion. That seems like a very big number to me and to Charlie Munger, Berkshire's vice chairman and my partner. (Should that number indeed prove too big, Charlie will find himself, in future reports, retrospectively identified as the senior partner.)' (Chairman's statement, Berkshire Hathaway Inc., 1988)

If your company has a performance record like Warren E Buffett's, *and* a chairman who is as willing – and as able – to set and express such clear objectives, you may argue that it does not need an IR manager.

But few companies – especially outside the USA – are blessed with chairmen who not only own such large blocks of their companies' shares but also recognize the rights of their co-owners to a long-sighted and – above all – understandable flow of information.

All too often, such rights are only acknowledged when the company desperately needs its shareholders' support. The result is a frantic search by head-hunters for someone to fill the gap, or a hasty briefing of PR consultants and advertising agencies to paper over the cracks.

The strategic planning director of a major drinks group recently said (publicly) that 'since it [IR] is purely concerned with giving our figures, we believe it must belong in the finance department', while a major pharmaceutical company speaker told a conference that 'we regard it as an integral part of the PR role'. No wonder both companies are rated below their competitors!

IR is neither purely the financial end of communication nor the communications end of finance. Rather, it is a direct responsibility of the board to report to their owners and they should ensure that this task is fulfilled as efficiently as every other. The intelligent board will recognize the strategic importance of the role as well as the need to allocate managerial resources to it.

Investors will normally expect the chairman or CEO to be responsible for keeping them informed – and so they should. The difficulty is that a non-executive chairman probably is not adequately informed and the CEO (whether chairman or MD) has to balance this responsibility with that of running the company. His colleagues, too, have their own principal roles to fulfil, while a junior executive may not have adequate knowledge of the facts, and almost certainly will not know all the background to them and *definitely* will not be accepted by senior fund managers as a suitable alternative to direct contact with his or her superiors.

International trends

In the USA, most chief executives of large, successful companies take the need for IR very seriously and have a very senior executive handling it – either on its own or combined with financial (often treasury), communications or marketing responsibilities.

Here in Europe, separate national securities markets, reinforced by exchange controls, have left few companies recognizing IR as an important part of overall strategy. This has resulted, all too often, in junior (often PR) executives or inadequately briefed consultants being given the job of 'improving our image in the City' or some similarly naive order – probably only when the company feels threatened.

Fund managers' views of IR

Not surprisingly, therefore, fund managers express mixed views about the value of IR as a whole, and about IR managers in particular. Our own (extensive) interviews bear out the results of a recent UK survey by Taylor Nelson/Equity International Magazine in this regard. In this first-ever survey of fund managers' attitudes to IR officers (IROs), Taylor Nelson/Equity International asked a selection of UK fund managers to answer a number of questions. Below are some of the results:

Are IROs the primary contact for fund managers?

	per cent
Yes	15
No	85

IROs offer a good alternative to contact with FDs or CEOs:

	per cent
Always	0
Sometimes	40
Never	60

IROs improve contact between fund managers and their company:

	per cent
Always	8
Sometimes	82
Never	10

Should more companies appoint designated IROs?

	per cent
Yes	40
No	55
Don't know	5

Source: Taylor Nelson/Equity International survey, April 1989.

Fund managers feel strongly that they need access to the company's senior management to judge its management team and to understand the background to corporate strategy. They therefore resent junior executives trying to block this access or to answer their questions without adequate knowledge and understanding. Many have encountered IR managers who were, in reality, PR managers and who proved useless to them – hence the negative reactions of some of them in the survey.

However, fund managers who had come across senior executives with specific IR responsibilities put those companies at the top of their lists of good communicators. They appreciated the availability of someone with a true understanding of company development, performance and strategy. They also said that the CEOs and FDs of these companies were usually no less available than in other companies but were able to stick to broader issues since the details had been dealt with separately.

Hence the 15 per cent of fund managers in the survey who regard IR managers as their primary contacts; the 40 per cent who said IR managers sometimes offer a good alternative to contact with FDs or CEOs; the 82 per cent who feel that IR managers sometimes improve their contact with the company; and the 40 per cent who believe that more companies should appoint designated IR managers.

Clearly, good IR managers are seen as very useful while poor ones are not only ineffective but may actually be a disadvantage. A further question in the survey perhaps sums it up:

How important are IROs as information providers?

	1st	2nd	3rd
Senior corporate officers	60	38	2
IR officers	2	57	5
Stockbrokers' analysts	38	5	93

Source: Taylor Nelson / Equity International survey, April 1989

The fund managers, in this survey and in our research, give high marks to those companies where they have a contact who is willingly available and is a senior manager, and where intelligent planning of shareholder contact is evident. They give almost equally low marks to those companies where no planned IR is evident and to those who appoint a junior executive to the task.

IR – a director's role?

The appointment of a board director – or, at least, a very senior manager – to the IR role, then, is the ideal from the investors' point of view and, given the strategic values that the company *can* derive from the role (see Chapter 1), probably from the company's viewpoint too.

Yet few European companies have so far placed enough importance upon the role of IR to make it a full-time responsibility at this level and, arguably, it is unlikely to be justifiable to do so except in companies with big international ambitions.

We conclude from this that IR is usually regarded as one of the responsibilities of a senior executive rather than as a full-time job. However, most companies considering the role for the first time are likely to under-estimate the amount of time required to handle it properly. Once you start to communicate with investors, it is crucial to keep going – remember, sporadic commitment to IR is worse than none at all. As your reputation for communicating improves, you will face increasing demands for contact.

In the active company, then, the IR role will demand more time than most directors can spare. One danger is that several directors will therefore be asked to share the role and the result will almost certainly be failure. It will not be clear to investors who the main contact is. What *will* be clear is that it is of secondary importance to all of them. The messages to *and* from investors are likely to be confused and – worst of all – there will be none of the clear planning and objective assessment which is a vital part of IR.

So what is the answer?

There is no clear-cut answer to the question of who should be responsible for a company's IR. Much will depend on the personalities and other responsibilities of its senior executives and on its likely need for future funding.

We have established that a senior executive must head the function – ideally a director, or a manager senior enough to attend management board or executive committee meetings. Investors need to know the explanations and reasoning behind performance and decisions, as well as the facts. If a full-time IR director cannot be justified, there are several alternatives and you need to examine the likely contenders and the qualities required.

Strategic marketing role?

In Chapter 1, we argued that IR is essentially about maintaining adequate – and orderly – demand for the company's securities at the best price which is consistent with its past and likely relative performance. This identifies IR as primarily a strategic marketing role. Therefore, like all marketing roles, it should not be done in isolation. The Japanese have best demonstrated the value of the team approach to strategic marketing, agreeing realistic long-term objectives, formulating comprehensive plans and expecting design, production, sales and marketing staff to work together.

Similarly, a successful IR programme will require teamwork between the chairman; the CEO; the finance, legal, communication and marketing teams; and, to some extent, the directors and managers of the company's operations.

But one person needs to act as the 'marketing director', taking the time to understand the needs and roles of the others and agree with them the objectives and plans. He – or his support team – will need to be able to spend a considerable amount of time in dealing with analysts and investors and in planning contact programmes involving the other executives.

We shall return to the qualities and responsibilities of this individual – who might come from another department or be appointed separately – but first, let's examine the contributions of the rest of the team.

The role of the chairman and the chief executive

How many of us would even consider sending out an untrained salesman to see grocery trade buyers whom he'd never met, with a sample of detergent whose market had never been researched, in packaging designed by an accountant, and with no prior advertising, no sales brochures and no point-of-sale display?

No-one (we hope). Yet this is precisely what many UK companies expect their chairman or CEO to do amongst the investment community. Many companies are highly skilled at marketing their products, yet they apply none of the accepted marketing principles to their shares.

Perhaps the problem is that no-one dare suggest that the 63-year-old chairman doesn't really *fully* understand his company's latest piece of technology, or the global potential of its next superdrug. Of course, the chairman understands what motivates the process engineer in Leeds to come to work every day in his Pitts Lane plant; after all, his company has excellent communications – the man gets the company newspaper every month and the chairman had a four-minute deep and meaningful conversation with him when he presented his silver jubilee medal four years ago.

Naturally, the chairman can put across this information better than anyone else; he's been doing it for the past 20 years! So how can you persuade him that his illustration of the management structure, drawn on a paper napkin, is not all that clear; he did, after all, try one of those new-fangled slide gizmos back in 1960. He's also getting a bit fed-up with the increasing proportion of fresh young analysts who turn up at the annual lunch. They keep asking such silly, detailed questions instead of listening to his overview; and he can't really admit he doesn't know the answer . . . but then the chairman's often quite good at waffling his way through . . . sometimes quite convincingly.

Many chairmen, chief executives and finance directors, of course, do make good ambassadors for the company and are fine communicators, but there are also plenty who do not. Since the majority of fund managers, brokers' analysts and financial media regard 'personal meetings with company's management' as the most important source of information on investments in UK companies, the lack of ability by senior management to communicate can prove a serious problem.

SOURCES OF INFORMATION ON INVESTMENTS IN UK COMPANIES (%)

	All	Fund Managers	Analysts	Journalists
BASE	75	40	25	10
Personal meetings with company's management	49	65	24	50
Press comment	43	20	68	70
Annual report and accounts / Interim results	39	33	40	60
Discussions with brokers and analysts	32	48	12	20
Analysts' reports	28	30	24	30
Computerized information services	24	18	36	20
Broker's lunches	23	30	12	20
Companies' news bulletins/ press releases	23	18	28	30
Presentations from companies' management	13	18	8	10
Corporate Press Advertising	12	10	16	10
Annual General Meeting	12	13	12	10
Word-of-mouth information	11	5	16	20
Industry and market reports	7	5	12	–
Corporate TV advertising	4	3	8	–
Take-over documents	3	–	4	10
Radio programmes	1	–	–	10

SOURCE: *Business Planning & Research International*

For those personal and larger meetings to be worthwhile they must be effective in imparting a coherent picture of the company's present and long-term prospects within its sector – both domestically and internationally – as well as the effects of the prevailing economic climate.

So what can chairmen and chief executives do to balance the demand for more direct information from the company at the most senior level, with their own job of running the business and their sometimes sadly lacking communications skills?

Although few of us are 'born communicators', some top executives are and training in communications can achieve a great deal in teaching executives to order their thoughts and select language which will make the principal messages of the company understandable, believable and attractive.

Chairmen and chief executives have often risen to the dizzy heights via accounting, engineering, scientific or legal routes which have not necessarily equipped them with the best communications skills. Undergoing a few rehearsals with practised trainers before major events, such as a results announcement, can prove invaluable, particularly in dealing with questions and answers.

The real value of such sessions is that they often show how unclear a company's strategy actually is. (There's nothing so educational as being forced to articulate the company's strategy, or the reason for its poor performance, in front of a video camera – and witnessing the full horror of the explanation's lack of conviction!) They also show up so-called strategies which, with the minimum of investigation, turn out to be just post-hoc rationalizations in management consultants' language for what they want to do anyhow. It's no good creating a high profile of your company's strategy unless you know what that strategy is.

Similarly, because a particular individual makes an excellent chairman of the board, it does not necessarily follow that he can string a sufficient number of written sentences together to provide a lucid chairman's statement for the annual report which gives a fair and accurate overview to the year's activities. More importantly the chairman is probably not that well attuned to the concerns of all of the shareholders – and if he is not addressing their needs, why is he bothering to write at all? Yet how many chairmen refuse to have one word of their archaic prose altered so that it makes an iota of sense to Mrs Bottlesham in Guildford who has £50,000 of her life savings tied up in the company? How many of them write a treatise on the global economy or the importance of interest rates – which Mrs Bottlesham prefers to get from the *Investors Chronicle*, and which adds nothing to her understanding of *her* company.

Some chairmen, of course, are very gifted at writing. Our friend Warren E Buffett of Berkshire Hathaway (see Chapter 1) uses the following simple prose to describe his company's management:

'Our premium of business value to book value has widened for simple reasons: we own some remarkable businesses and they are run by even more remarkable managers.

'You have a right to question the second assertion. After all, CEOs seldom tell their shareholders that they have assembled a bunch of turkeys to run things. Their reluctance to do so makes for some strange annual reports. Oftentimes, in his shareholders' letter, a CEO will go on for pages detailing corporate performance that is woefully inadequate. He will nonetheless end with a warm paragraph describing his managerial comrades as "our most precious assets". Such comments sometimes make you wonder what the other assets can possibly be.'

Later, mixing humour with honesty, Mr Buffet presents a detailed picture of the performance of his company's diverse range of activities (the average as well as the exceptional) which is understandable and enjoyable to everyone from the least financially-literate private shareholder to the most analytical of all fund managers. For example, accompanying a table of clear financial detail and explanatory text, he says:

'Gypsy Rose Lee announced on one of her later birthdays: "I have everything I had last year; its just that its all two inches lower". As this table shows, during 1987 almost all of our business aged in a more upbeat way.'

The chairman's statement was never intended to be exclusively as a personal opportunity to discuss life, Plato and the universe. It is meant to be a short introduction to the director's report, aimed at the owners of the business – all of them. So unless the chairman is an excellent writer and has an unusually good grasp of the business, he should invite help from others. He might be well-advised to pass the job to people inside or outside the company who specialize in communicating and who, with adequate briefing from the chairman, will be able to produce a first draft which ensures that the annual report becomes the essential communications tool it is supposed to be: clear, informative and credible.

After all, few chairmen would insist on writing their own TV commercials – the £75,000 production cost alone would deter them from such a waste of company money. Yet the annual report will probably cost over £100,000 to produce; it's aimed at an equally – if not more – crucial audience; and that audience is unlikely to even look at the rest of the book if the chairman's statement strikes them as pompous, poorly written, or, worst of all, irrelevant.

As for personal appearances, there is certainly no requirement for either the chairman or the chief executive to attend each analyst briefing or every presentation to fund managers – any more than they would attend every sales call on customers. Indeed, there is a strong argument that they shouldn't because it takes them away from running the business. Many of these briefings and presentations can be handled by the finance director and the IR manager.

They certainly are required, however, at the AGM and for the announcement of the interim and final results, as well as for giving briefings in special circumstances, such as a new share issue or takeover.

The chief executive must demonstrate a firm and full grip, with all the details, of the company's activities, its current performance, future prospects and the reason, say, for the rights issue; and must be able to convey this information clearly and convincingly. The chairman should usually restrict himself to giving an overview which puts the chief executive's remarks into context and which indicates the board's solid approval for the actions of the chief executive (or, if they do not approve his plans, their plan to replace the chief executive!).

Institutional investors, brokers' analysts, and the financial media have an expectation *not* to be able to get hold of either the company chairman or chief executive at a moment's notice. Indeed, it is almost certainly inadvisable that they should be able to reach the chairman, if he is non-executive, because he won't be up-to-date with day-to-day developments within the company. And how come the chief executive is so instantly accessible, if he is meant to be running the company? Fund managers, and even financial journalists, are perfectly content to deal with the person charged with the IR function, provided he is knowledgeable and reliable – and therefore credible – and provided they know that they will be able to get the chairman or chief executive if it *is* appropriate.

The chairman and chief executive must also be prepared to devote time to 'roadshows' – presentations to fund managers and analysts in countries where the company already has, or is planning, a listing.

Employees should not be neglected either, particularly where the company offers share options and Save As You Earn schemes. They also represent owners of the company and are likely to remain amongst the more loyal in difficult situations.

So the role of the executive chairman or chief executive is to agree the overall objectives, strategy and IR programme which will usually have been worked out by the finance, legal and communications special-ists. He needs to decide who in the organization has the most appropri-ate communications skills and who already possesses – or can develop – the necessary level of financial and company knowledge to drive the programme; respond to day-to-day questions from investors, analysts, and the financial media; and give personal advice and market feedback on which he can rely.

The chief executive must be prepared to devote personal time to the 'big' occasions, such as the results or a 'special' situation; and have a firm, articulate grip on all the facts as well as a credible view on the imponderables.

Ultimately, he must be able to demonstrate a clearly-focused business strategy for the company which fulfils the requirements of its shareholders and which will gain widespread acceptance in the marketplace.

These are no mean tasks to achieve and do not happen overnight. Messages about the company's current performance and its future aspirations need hammering home constantly. Chief executives and those responsible for running the IR programme must resist the temptation of becoming bored with the process, believing that because they have delivered the message a couple of times, the job has been done. The same effort that went into the first presentation should be there at the twentieth.

Since financial audiences do not expect the chief executive to be accessible at the drop of a hat, the appointment of a suitably qualified individual to act as the day-to-day interface with the financial community, and keep the programme on schedule, helps develop confidence in the company and its strategic direction. Such an appointment also demonstrates the importance which the CEO attaches to the need for effective two-way financial communications. Watch the share prices of companies who have just appointed IR managers – the rise is probably more to do with the new, more communicative, approach by the CEO than it is to do with anything the IR manager could do in his first few months.

The finance director

The finance director (FD) who claims sole rights over the IR function because it is primarily about financing the company, is like the technical director who argues in favour of giving a car sales dealership to a back-street dealer because he has the best workshops.

The FD's role in the IR process, though, is absolutely critical. He needs to be available to meet institutional investors, brokers' analysts and the financial media on a regular basis: financial controls are unquestionably a key feature of the company. He must also ensure that whoever is doing the day-to-day IR has the right answers available at their disposal, and must be able to deputize for the chief executive at results time – especially if the company is listed on more than one stock exchange. For example, he may need to be in New York to lead presentations while the chief executive leads those in London.

However, an unplanned programme can waste time – he can end

up seeing analysts who have no influence or fund managers who met the CEO last week. In a well-planned IR programme, the FD can spend just as much time (and may well be persuaded by the IR manager to spend more) but it will be used more effectively.

Individuals in the FD's department also have a vital role to play: providing the IR function with operating data such as results and the effects of prices, volumes and market share on lines of business, as well as data on external influences like the effect of high oil prices, bad weather, lower interest rates and so on.

The FD and his colleagues need to be intimately involved in the IR function (especially if it sits outside the FD's own department) so that data can be collated, strategic messages built-up for transmission to the investment community, and an intelligent reception given to any messages that come back.

He should also be amenable to the fact that some financial training will be desirable if the IR manager's background is essentially communication or marketing but, equally, some communication and marketing training will be in order if a finance specialist is given the IR role.

However, the FD who tries to handle IR without assistance has the disadvantage that he cannot say 'I don't know' in reply to a financial question. He is faced with answering immediately (always dangerous given that his head may be filled with figures which should not be disclosed and may not have had time to consider the implications behind the question) or refusing to answer and thus appearing uncooperative.

The competent FD will always welcome someone who can say 'I don't know but I'll find out' and hence win the company time to consider all the implications before answering. This assumes that the company has avoided choosing the traditional kind of PR person, who would never admit a lack of knowledge but would *ad lib* through an answer, often leaving an incorrect (and probably dangerously so) impression in the market.

The rewards will be felt when, as so often happens, those in the accounting function become so involved in their own complex processes that they lose sight of the fact that they are responsible for providing shareholders with understandable financial reports on the company's progress. These reports may, of course, be understandable to themselves and their fraternity but are double-Dutch to Mrs Bottlesham in Guildford who only wants to know what is happening to her £50,000.

Communications professionals, with the right amount of financial grounding can not only translate the double-Dutch into English but can also prevent a major misconception arising about the company because some item has been badly expressed.

Integration of financial knowledge and communications skills applies equally to the preparation of takeover or merger documentation and to dealings with rating agencies (see Chapter 6 on credit ratings). Companies meet with these agencies on a regular basis, reporting to them on key issues like projected cash flow, coverage ratios and implications of strategic plans, as they affect a company's ability to service its debt.

Although presentations to the ratings agencies often contain material confidential to the company, and are in no way designed to help sell securities directly, the information given to the credit rating agencies remains confidential to them, and the need to communicate effectively with them is crucial because of their influence with investors.

In difficult financial periods, companies quickly realize that debt holders (whose lending decisions and interest rates are governed by the 'debt worthiness' rating given by the agencies) come before preferred or common shareholders. Recapitalization normally requires debtholder consent and, in a worst case scenario of bankruptcy, the debtholders call the shots. Furthermore, convertible shares, leveraged buyouts, and so on, are blurring the distinction between equity and debt.

Yet finance directors often keep debtholder relations outside the remit of the IR function; some IR managers are kept unaware of their existence, and are given no opportunity to review the material for communications sense before it is presented – a lack of integration which might damage the company's chances of achieving its financial objectives. And we have all seen the effect on companies' equity when their debt ratings are reduced!

In summary, it is a mistake for the FD to view the IR process simply as a means of facilitating the financial activity he believes to be right for the company's future expansion. He can *expect* to do so – provided the IR programme has encompassed all the disciplines of the marketing process and he has taken into account the views and needs of the market to be addressed before making any moves.

Indeed, a good IR manager is more likely to be persuading the FD to make more appearances than less, just as the good sales director will find the technical director a useful asset at sales presentations.

Whoever is ultimately given the job, the financial team must integrate their financial knowledge with marketing and communications skills to ensure that the IR process becomes a continuous and effective one, irrespective of the level of financial activity taking place at any particular moment.

The company secretary

The company secretary, or 'legal director', also has a critical, but often much under-used, role in the integrated IR process.

Responsible for keeping the company on the legal straight and narrow and for shareholder services and records, the company secretary should have an enormous input in maintaining an updated and accurate register of shareholder interests in the company.

Regrettably, it is only in recent years, spurred on by the spate of unwelcome takeover bids in the Eighties, that the importance of maintaining an accurate and balanced share register has been recognized. Faced, sometimes, with huge workloads, and the need for consistent detailed technical accuracy, few company secretaries have felt the inclination to embark on a detailed analysis of shareholdings accumulated over long periods of time.

Usually what changes that perspective is the unwanted takeover bid, when tens of thousands of pounds are spent in a couple of weeks with outside firms to develop information that could have been available from the company's own office right from the start.

The company secretary's role has not been helped either by the apathy of share registrars – organizations which offer to maintain the share register on the company's behalf, and act as a mailbox when communicating with shareholders.

A survey of the share registration market undertaken in 1988 by Katrina Ellis of The London Business School shows that, while companies are waking up to the fact that having quick access to the current status of the share register can be vitally important, and something for which they would pay a premium, few registrars are capitalizing on this and most continue to offer traditional services that show they are largely unaware of such developments.

In the past, share registration was largely a non-profit making activity, offered as a 'loss leader' to attract clients to more lucrative services such as accounting or corporate finance.

Simple lists of names and addresses are, however, of little value to organizations who require detailed analysis of investor demographics – the company's single most powerful source of information on market segmentation. (See Chapter 3 on defining the audience.)

As well as being the keeper of the shareholder register, with or without the help of a registrar, the company secretary is responsible for producing the legal documentation that surrounds the financial activity undertaken by the company – *which, by definition, has to be made understandable to the investment community.*

In most companies, he will act as the compliance officer and, sometimes, the corporate conscience. Certainly, if the company has multiple share listings or makes frequent share issues, the compliance role is a complex one – and one that must inter-relate carefully with the IR function.

Furthermore, it will traditionally be the company secretary who receives complaints from the authorities about the company's failure to make a timely announcement; who will be advised by the lawyers about the impact of the latest change to the Companies Act; or who will be consulted by the Securities Industry Committee about the importance to the company of private shareholders. These are all IR – as well as regulatory – concerns.

Part of the company secretary's training in techniques for keeping the company out of the courts will have been in the use of legal English which is technically specific and absolutely unambiguous when read by a judge or fellow lawyer. Terms are defined in excruciating detail and attached to short-hand labels that are then used in quotes throughout the legal document (eg, 'the company', 'the merger').

The problem here is that neither investors nor the financial media have had the same kind of training so, once again, people with communications skills are often needed to decipher this legalese and turn it into plain English for press releases and scripts for presentations surrounding relevant announcements. Clearly, this will be a much simpler process if the corporate communications department has worked closely with the company secretary from the outset of each project.

So, in the IR process, the company secretary's role is: to ensure that the share register is kept up-to-date and designed to provide information about shareholder demographics at great speed when needed; to keep those in the IR team informed of significant changes on the register; to ensure that the IR process complies with all of the regulations – at home and abroad – that apply; and to co-operate with the IR team when putting together legal documentation so that plain English versions for wider distribution, as well as the meeting of legal requirements, can be developed in parallel and not at the eleventh minute of the eleventh hour.

The predator detector

Current information on share movements to identify stakebuilders is increasingly at a premium.

During April 1987, a stake of 3.5 per cent was built in Courtaulds. Citicorp Vickers made the initial purchases to disguise the identity of the real buyer – Mr Kerry Packer.

After a stream of small purchases, the shares were transferred to a security account in two separate blocks during overnight trading. Brokers were aware of these large transactions but were unable to determine their destination.

The *Sunday Times* reported on 1 May: 'Courtaulds itself took some time to react. It fired off enquiries about the Scrimgeour purchases on April 21 using its powers under the Companies Act to learn the beneficial ownership of shares held in nominee accounts.'

Research by Addition – one of several companies which attempt to fill the niche left open by registrars by investigating, interpreting and displaying a company's register – shows that in 80 per cent of bids, the stake-builder tests the water before launching a full-scale bid.

The company examines the whole register rather than just the week or month's-end balance. This means they would have been able to detect the small purchases made by Mr Packer before the brokers, who only noticed when the shares were transferred in larger blocks. They monitor movements and trigger 212 letters (so called because they fall under section 212 of the Companies Act) to force nominee account disclosure through an automatic 'predator detector' option in their software.

Qualities needed by an IR manager

It is clear, then, that the in-house manager responsible for the IR role – whether he has a whole department or sits in another department and uses outside consultants – must be close enough to the people running the company (or be one of them) to be able to interpret facts and events properly on the company's behalf. The PR person who reports to the head of personnel, who then reports to the company secretary, will probably never win the analysts' confidence and will annoy them by trying to interpose between them and the people who do know what's going on.

He must be available, to a reasonable degree, for the dozens of day-to-day questions that arise, as well as for major events like the announcement of interim and final results.

He must be reliable, in terms of getting hold of answers not immediately available, but should be knowledgeable – at least about overall policy and strategy, if not about where every penny went in the Source and Applications of Funds statement.

Financial, company and sector knowledge are essential pre-requisites for the job but can be acquired through experience. The real skills required are the abilities to communicate and to persuade. Without these, how can the IR manager hope to convince financial audiences about the appropriateness of the actions being taken by the company, or convince the company's own management about actions it needs to take to convey the messages which support the company's strategy?

The messages designed for the IR programme – which in turn have been evolved out of the objectives of the programme and the audiences for whom they are intended – must be consistent with all the messages being transmitted by all parts of the company to all of its audiences.

The ability of all parts of the company to sing off the same hymn sheet is crucial to its credibility, and designing and co-ordinating corporate messages which accurately reflect the overall business objectives and strategy of the company should be the result of serious discussion between communications specialists and senior operational, financial and legal management.

Whether an organization employs individuals able to fulfil that role usually reflects the way in which it views the role of communications in the first place, either short-term and tactical (the ability to soften the impact of bad news or spreading the glitter on even modest good news) or as part of the corporate strategic planning process.

IR answers back

In the US, the president of a major corporate division presented a convoluted, ill-advised acquisition scheme to the heads of corporate staff departments. In his division, communications were used strictly for short-term and tactical purposes. When he finished, he turned to the head of corporate communications and said: 'Once this whore is ready to go, I want you to dress her up and take her to the dance'. He fully expected an enthusiastic response, complete with comments on appropriate press interviews, brochures, speeches and so on. In his division, that's exactly what would have happened.

At corporate level, however, things were quite different. The head of corporate communications began to ask a series of pointed questions that exposed serious problems with the scheme. He knew his company's business. He knew its investors and their advisors. He knew what they would accept and what they would question, and why.

He was trained in law, as well as grounded in finance, and had 20 years' experience in communications. By the time he had finished, the project was, quite properly, dead in the water.

An extreme example perhaps, but one that clearly illustrates how management's expectations affect the depth of involvement of the communications function in any company. At corporate level, management clearly expected, and received, much more

---

substantive involvement from this function than was the case at the division in question. In fact, as a result of this meeting, the chief executive of the corporation took a personal interest in changing attitudes in that division.

Driving the IR programme has to be a co-ordinated team effort between the communications, finance and company secretary's departments because all have an important contribution to make. The individual who runs the programme on a day-to-day basis must be a communicator with marketing, financial and company knowledge, irrespective of whose department he sits in.

Once the appointment is made, the individual should be named in all publications, including the accounts, to give the investment community a specific point of reference. We could take a lesson from the French here: the Paris Bourse actually requires every listed company to nominate an official spokesperson for the company.

The external consultant

In his book *How the Stock Markets Work* (Hutchinson Business 1988), Colin Chapman points out that it is often the City public relations firm which oils the wheels of the information industry.

'Financial public relations companies,' he says, 'like to think they are a cut above their contemporaries in the West End of London who deal with products and services, and they probably are. Their senior people certainly behave better, and have larger expense accounts.'

Without giving anything away about the expense accounts, the external communications consultant certainly has a role to play – but, ultimately, the consultant can only be as effective as the IR manager who drives him from within the client organization.

The good ones can help to be the eyes and ears for companies in feeding back information on shareholders' opinion, what the media are saying and, increasingly important, providing an assessment of Whitehall and EC opinion. They can generate new ideas; provide 'best advice' in relation to current IR practice; advise on the rules and regulations surrounding the disclosure of financial information; bring technical know-how to making presentations; and produce 'arms and legs' support for busy situations.

If the client-consultancy relationship develops successfully, consultants can become sufficiently close to the key client organization to be able to script many of the key presentations and printed material, with the minimum of briefing and the maximum degree of accuracy.

However, both the client and the consultancy must be prepared to devote enough time to allow the consultancy to develop such a close relationship if it is to offer strategic communications advice specific to the organization and provide 'behind the scenes' assistance with programme implementation. This can only happen if the chemistry between client and consultant is right.

Consultants should not be used, however, as the over-voice of the company since, although they might be able to represent it, they are clearly *not* of it and the client organization's credibility will be damaged as a result. Furthermore, many of the City PR firms have spotted IR as the fastest-growing area of communication and some who would not know the difference between ROE and RPM are now claiming IR expertise. Those, however, with genuine, regular contacts with analysts and the financial media, usually for a broad range of clients, can prove invaluable in feeding back information and providing direction for future strategies. But even they will only incite resentment if they prevent – or appear to be trying to prevent – direct contact between the company's management and its owners.

Some IR consultancies have spotted the niche created by the failure of many of the share registrar firms to offer effective share tracking systems, and now offer their own (see Outside help? on page 44).

So who *should* hold the short straw?

In conclusion, then, given that there is no single answer, what are the key factors in deciding who should have the responsibility of IR?

- The CEO must take the final rap.
- A senior corporate officer should have specific IR responsibility.
- Financial, legal, marketing and communication staff must co-operate.
- The IR manager should ideally report directly to the CEO to ensure the IR manager's internal and external credibility and to avoid excessive influence on the process by finance, legal or other staff, and to ensure that emphasis remains on long-term strategy – and not on second- or third-hand versions of what needs to be done.
- Finance directors can be too numbers-oriented and not sufficiently aware of the company's non-financial strengths (and weaknesses). If they have the job, the CEO should insist on non-financial IR support staff.
- Company secretaries are often too legalistic and conservative. They may not be able to put across a 'feel' for the company and will probably need financial and marketing support staff.
- Marketing directors and PR people may be too inclined to 'hype'

the company. The CEO should ensure that financial and legal input is maintained.
- Consultants should be just that – they should not be allowed to undermine the company's relationship with its owners.

CHAPTER 3

They're only the owners
– defining and segmenting the audience

'Then the guy from the Church Commissioners put his hand up and asked about pay rates in our South African operations and the boss started to get rattled.

"Why on earth did you invite them to the lunch?"

"Well, I read that they're one of the country's largest funds." '

Companies with large South African operations inviting the Church Commissioners to a presentation; firms with defence interests approaching left-wing union pension funds; and fast-growing high-tech outfits targeting income trusts, without recognizing their different information needs, deserve the scorn they often provoke.

Sending the chairman to a lunch with fund managers without heavy research first is equivalent to sending your salespeople to call on potential customers without briefing them on what business they already do with your firm, what products they might need and how your products would meet those needs compared with competing products; in fact, its even worse – at least the salespeople might have some training and experience in the job.

Fear or strategy

Whether the decision to improve the company's IR is driven by fear of takeover or by more strategic considerations, it has to start with research. The company needs to know who owns its shares and the objectives of those owners.

If takeover is a concern, the company will need to be able to detect suspicious purchases and identify the key people who will make – or influence – the decision upon which its future depends. It may well need to reach these people at very short notice.

If the programme is more strategic in nature, proper research will be necessary to define the existing *and potential* market for the shares (or other securities), to design messages appropriate to both markets and the company, and to monitor the programme's effectiveness. To define the audience accurately, you have to go back to one of the first principles of marketing – segmentation. Many different groups will have acquired shares in your company, or may be thinking about doing so, but their reasons for making the purchase will vary enormously.

Rolls-Royce or Bedford?

When a consumer selects one packet of washing powder over another, the selection is made because the product is perceived to meet the consumer's needs. The perception which prompted the purchase is created through a variety of messages targeted at the consumer to encourage precisely the purchase that is eventually made. As Johnnie D Johnson, executive vice president of Georgeson & Company (an IR company in the US which recently linked with City and Commercial in London) put it, segmentation of share ownership rarely goes beyond the following two basic points:

1. Some investors are primarily dividend-orientated; some are primarily growth-orientated; some seek a balance of each in the same security. (This is like saying some people buy cars, some buy trucks and some buy estate cars.)
2. The 'market' is divided between institutions and individuals. (This is the same as saying vehicles are generally bought by either businesses or households.)

As Mr Johnson points out, not all businesses and households buy identical cars, trucks or estate cars. The purchase decision depends on their own personal needs, the budget available, perceptions of the product and fashion trends. Those same criteria apply to buying shares.

Start on yourself

The first step is to look at the company's own current and likely future performance characteristics. These, to a large extent, will dictate the kinds of investor who will be best suited to, and attracted to, the shares of the company which you are trying to market. In fact, to carry the car analogy further, some researchers actually ask investors whether they see your company as a Rolls-Royce, a mini, a Porsche or a Volvo

– it can be a fascinating way to see how they feel, as well as what they know, about your business.

If the company is on the defensive (it may be going through a major restructuring of its businesses, or new management may have been brought in to sort out problems) it is likely to want shareholders who are in for the long ride, either private or big institutions who are looking for income and long-term capital appreciation.

On the other hand, a company which is in an expansionist phase will require, and be more suited to, more volatile investors who come in and out of the stock so pushing up trading volume, keeping the share price up, and allowing the company to pursue its expansionist plans. Indeed, the first consideration for a company in this position will be whether equities or debt offer the most favourable route to achieving its objectives.

Usually there will be special factors which affect this kind of decision. For example, highly-geared companies in the service industry will be looking hard at acquiring new equity whereas a company which has a low gearing, because it has withdrawn from a few markets, will find debt more attractive.

Understand your customers

Then there are the fund's characteristics. It is relatively simple to establish whether they tend to sit on stocks or move in and out over short periods of time. Another characteristic may be their sense of ethical values: if the company has operations in South Africa, or is part of the defence or cigarette industries, for example, there will be some investors who won't touch it with a bargepole – so there will be little point in targeting them.

Some funds turn over 60 per cent of their portfolio every year in a (usually vain) attempt to beat the indices; others are totally index-linked, so they don't even want to hear from you – if your shares make up 2 per cent of the index, they'll own 2 per cent, no matter what. Some funds are wholly self-managed; others are entirely managed by a third party (or two or more). Some have their own research analysts; others depend on brokers.

In any case, if your company is going to consolidate in a very stable market, there will be no point targeting high-growth funds; if you are going to sell your manufacturing units and acquire service businesses you're wasting your time going after a fan of assets and gearing. You *must* use executive time efficiently.

Secondary reasons for analyzing the share register and altering the balance of its ownership may include a decision to encourage share ownership by employees or because of some glaring imbalance in the company's present ownership. There is an encouraging trend towards employee share ownership because employees tend to remain supportive and loyal, particularly during difficult times. Employee share ownership schemes can also provide an effective means for the company to introduce new working practices, if the two are offered simultaneously.

Imbalances in the share register may mean too few of the right institutions holding shares in the company – or no shares at all; or too few or too many private shareholders. Too many private shareholders has certainly become a problem for some of the recently privatized industries who own only a handful of stock but, nonetheless, require the same expensive, statutory, servicing as much larger shareholders. (In the US, the problem of too many private shareholders is being overcome by companies' legal right to buy back such shareholdings on favourable terms to the investor, known as 'odd lot buy backs', but there is little evidence of this catching on in Britain.)

The percentage of shares owned by individuals fell from roughly 65 per cent 30 years ago to 28 per cent in 1981, and to about 20 per cent now. While government privatizations have brought a lot of new individual investors into the market, there is considerable doubt about whether the trend has been stopped, let alone reversed.

The everchanging backdrop

When defining and segmenting the audience for the IR programme, consideration also needs to be given to the everchanging backdrop to making investment decisions. Increasing globalization of the market, the growth in index-linked investment and the control of equities shrinking into fewer and fewer hands should all be causes of concern to a company's management since all these factors may contribute to increasing short-term investment decisions and pressure on companies to perform over the short term.

The trend towards securitization of debt (issuing paper to lenders which can then be freely traded, eg, bonds and commercial paper), the question of whether or not to add in brand values to the balance sheet, and the move towards global and EEC harmonization of regulations are all part of the shifting background to the IR process.

Changes in the role of the 'middlemen' – the brokers, who are being regarded with increasing suspicion by their traditional clientele – the fund managers; the nomadic existence of the financial press who switch publications and areas of specialization with alarming frequency; and the great coming of TAURUS all help to make plotting the IR path about as straightforward as following Italian politics.

Then there is the need to ensure co-ordination of corporate messages to each of the company's audiences: each message may need dressing-up in different language but they all need to say the same thing. There's no point in having one set of messages for the investment community ('we know where we're going, our strategy is in place, our products are market leaders and margins are rising') and another set for employees ('things are going to be really tough, productivity is shot to hell, we can't compete in today's markets'), especially if you're about to launch an Employee Share Option Scheme (ESOPS), thus removing the distinction between staff and shareholders.

Before edging your way across these shifting sands, you have to be crystal clear about what the IR programme is designed to achieve and the strategy which is going to get you there. And you must have sufficient in-built flexibility to adapt the programme when outside forces dictate.

Beginning the search

In analyzing the company's share register, two major frustrations are certain to be encountered. The first is the length of time it takes for registered shareholders to actually appear on the register; and when they do, the number which appears under nominee names.

Since a share register can hold anything from a few hundred to several million names, like British Telecom's, conducting the analysis can be a very long job and may require some outside assistance. The first level of information you need is that of individuals registered under their own name. This can be provided by the company's registrar and can then be taken out of the analysis for the time being.

Similarly, the registrar will be able to let you have the names of institutional investors registered under their own name – so they too can temporarily be put to one side until you're ready to feed them into the IR programme itself.

The majority of shareholders, however, will be registered under nominee names – usually to save them from storing and administering hundreds of share certificates and all of the forms involved in trading. Furthermore, the register will be constantly changing and the present system is very slow to feed these changes through (see Share transfers – the current UK system, below), with registrars often not able to let you know who your new registered owner is until four – six weeks after he bought his shares.

All change – TAURUS

At long last, the system is about to change. London is to move to rolling settlement instead of ten-day trading periods, so registrars should receive details of all transactions within five days. A new computer system, codenamed TAURUS, is to be introduced to improve the

Share transfers – the current UK system

Currently, if a shareholder wants to sell some or all of his shares, he notifies a broker who does the trade through a market-maker (in his own firm or elsewhere). The market-maker's back office should, by the next day, enter the sale into the Stock Exchange Talisman computer, which transfers ownership of the shares into his own nominee company – SEPON (Stock Exchange Pool Nominee Limited). Meanwhile, the market-maker acting for the buyer also enters the transaction into Talisman and the computer checks that the details match. The shares are then held in a SEPON suspense account until the next day (six working days after the end of each ten-day dealing period), when the selling market-maker should receive the seller's share certificate and signed transfer, and the buying market-maker should receive the buyer's payment. Talisman now transfers the shares from SEPON to the buyer and notifies the company's registrar – usually six–21 days after the trade took place. The negotiator will enter the new holder on the register and send off the new share certificate.

The new UK system – TAURUS

Early proposals for the new TAURUS computer include several key features which should be introduced during 1990:
- Rolling settlement to replace the old ten-day trading periods.
- The introduction of separate computer accounts for the main City 'players', so that they could maintain details of ownership directly on the computer – which would make it possible for them to show all beneficial interests in each nominee holding, although it is not yet clear whether they will be obliged or encouraged to provide such helpful transparency of ownership.
- A listed company advisory service (LCAS) which will be responsible for answering requests from companies or their registrars about ownership of their shares. It is not yet clear that the LCAS will prove to have been designed with a proper appreciation of the likely volume of company enquiries, or what the companies will be charged for this service.
- The possibility of 'dematerialization' – ie, a change in the law requiring the issue of a share certificate as legal proof of ownership.

settlement and registration methods – and possibly to allow for the abolition of share certificates as legal proof of ownership. However, as we discussed in Chapter 1, it is not yet clear whether this will make ownership more or less transparent, or what service will be available, at what cost.

Storage – the ubiquitous database

As the answers come in, they need to be logged into a computer database and tied in with the names of the original nominees so a picture builds up of who acts as nominee to whom. Additional information will need to be added to the database later, such as that on people actually controlling or advising on those funds which they don't own themselves. You may also want to add in the names of brokers to track the degree of their influence on investment decisions.

The computer database should store:

- details of registered private and institutional shareholders
- nominee holdings and the beneficial owners they represent
- details of links with fund managers, advisers and brokers.

Later, when the IR programme is underway, it will be important to add in records of meetings and other IR activity as well as the names of individual institutional fund managers in order to invite them to briefings and presentations as the programme develops.

Outside help?

All of this represents a fair task and you may decide to employ external assistance to analyze the register fully. The company's registrar, as we saw in Chapter 2, is unlikely to be able to help beyond the early, easy stages of revealing actual registered shareholders, but there are specialist firms whose lives are dedicated to such activity.

The best-known is probably Technimetrics. One of the services it provides is the supply, either on computer tape, or paper, or address labels, of lists of all the major institutions and different levels of individuals within them, including the name of the boss, fund managers and analysts in specific sectors. (Technimetrics' US list is good and its European one improving all the time.)

A number of other companies have spotted the niche and make various claims to providing similar – or complementary – services. They include financial public relations specialists, such as City & Commercial, and Carter Valin Pollen, other firms of specialist consultants and some brokers too (as a service to their corporate clients) – most notably Cazenove.

Great care, however, should be exercised in deciding whom to

employ as external help. The three crucial questions to ask are:
- How much will it cost?
- Which clients may I talk to for references?
- How much information can I have instant access to?

Peeling the onion

Once you have the information on *registered* holder's, you can begin the laborious process of peeling away the nominee names to try to find out two pieces of information: the names of the end-owners of the stock who are controlling their own investment decisions, and the names of those companies managing funds on behalf of others who may or may not be a link in the ownership chain. For example, a firm like Phillips and Drew Fund Management, as well as holding share certificates in their own right, will be advising and/or controlling funds on behalf of other companies and individuals.

The principal method for determining ownership of nominee holdings in the UK is to send a letter to each nominee holder, requiring him – under Section 212 of The Companies Act – to disclose, within 28 days, the identity of the company or individual in whose name the shares are being held. If the holder does not comply, his or her voting rights can be withdrawn. A new Stock Exchange rule will cut the disclosure period to 14 days and allow an additional penalty of non-compliance – withholding of dividends. Of course, if it is a multi-layer nominee holding, you need to trigger-off another 212 letter for each layer until you get to the bottom of the cascade – which can delay the eventual disclosure of the controlling owner for several months!

Sinister holdings

The UK disclosure requirements are due to change with the 1989 Finance Act. Clause 108 will require all holders of three per cent of a company's shares to disclose their holdings within three days (previous limits were five per cent and five days). The takeover requirements have also been tightened up to allow only 24 hours for the notification of every one per cent acquired once a bid has been declared.

Disclosure rules in other countries vary from five per cent in the USA and France to 25 percent in West Germany. But the EEC has declared that it seeks 'market transparency so that investors can take informed decisions'; an EEC commission proposal would require all members to make disclosure mandatory at ten per cent by 1990.

(With regard to this last question, a common criticism of Cazenove, for example, is that while it will target the right people for you and get them to, say, a meeting, it will not let you have copies of the actual lists.)

DIY analysis

The whole process of analyzing the register and keeping its records up-to-date is really not that complicated for a large data-processing organization. While most companies may need some outside help, a larger company should at least consider maintaining its own records on its top 100 shareholders internally. Both Consgold and BP would have saved themselves a good deal of embarrassment if they had had their share register analysis systems properly up and running.

Revealed – the owners

So now, perhaps two or three months after you began the process of analyzing the register, depending upon the amount of resources you put into the operation, you should have a fairly clean list of private and institutional owners, both in their own names and the ones uncovered, together with details of who advises them, which brokers they use, and who manages the funds (if they are not self-managed) plus names and addresses.

The list of private shareholders may not be quite as clean because 212 letters will simply have revealed that a particular firm of portfolio fund managers has, for example, '432 private shareholders holding 12,352 shares in your company's stock'. But it almost certainly isn't worth the time and trouble of breaking these shareholders down further. The individual shareholders may not know, or have forgotten, that they are shareholders in your company, and you can add their names and addresses easily later if you send out a circular (via the nominees) which encourages a direct reply – eg, a shareholder perk offer.

To obtain an even more detailed profile on private shareholders, the register itself can be postcoded, so that the list of shareholders can be broken down on a regional basis – which can prove useful in targeting regional advisors and newspapers, and deciding where to hold regional shareholder meetings. Then, external research firms can be used to find out information such as origin and length of shareholding, age, sex and other demographic details.

Employees

Because of the increasing importance of employees as shareholders it is as important to track their level of financial involvement with the company as it is for other individual investors. If you do not have complete staff lists (eg, payroll) good basic lists can be obtained through pension or ESOP schemes. Running these lists against private shareholder lists will show how many employees are individual shareholders in their own right. Having such information, provided that the findings are reasonably impressive, can impress other investors.

So, too, will directors' holdings. Institutions like to know if directors are putting their money where their mouths are. A number of outfits

Turnover of UK equity by institutions

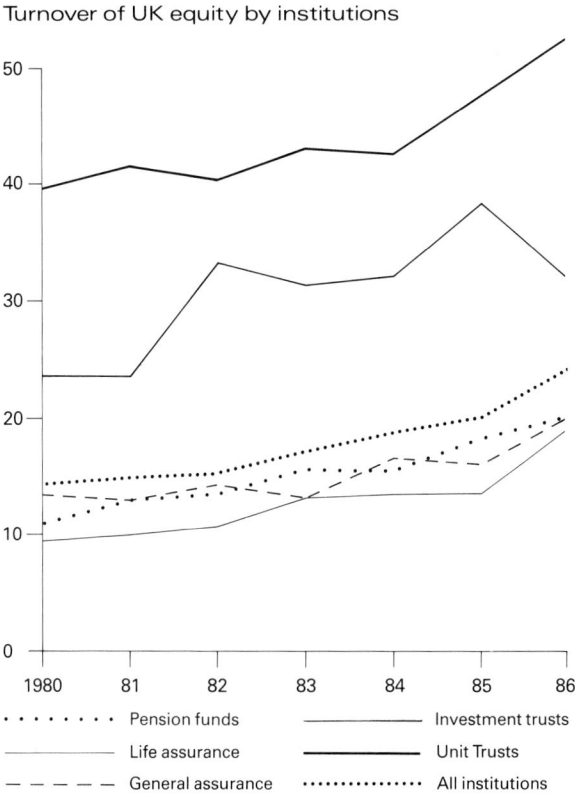

· · · · · · · ·	Pension funds	————————	Investment trusts
————————	Life assurance	————————	Unit Trusts
— — — — —	General assurance	·················	All institutions

Source: Wood Mackenzie and Co Ltd.

Note: turnover is defined as sales plus purchases of equity, less net investment,divided by two (for each sale there is an equivalent purchase).

Figure 1

circulate details of share buying and selling by directors of PLCs (which must, of course, be announced) and investors set great store by these. They don't always appreciate, however, that directors' share options are usually given to them and that they often sell some of these to buy the remainder – so their dealings aren't always as indicative as they seem at first sight.

Institutions

So far, we have found only the names of the institutional shareholders and we will need to learn much more about the individuals who control and influence them, and about their policies.

There are numerous ways to do this, none of them particularly complicated. Use members of your department, or bring in an undergraduate during his summer holidays to go through reference material such as the *Investment Trust Yearbook*, *Crawfords Directory*, *Becket's* and *Who's Who in the City of London* together with brochures and annual reports of the large institutions, to discover approximately how much the institutions are investing in the UK equities market and compare it with the percentage they hold of your own stock and you'll get an indication of the 'light' holders as well as the non-holders who could be worth pursuing.

This exercise should also give you a good indication of the investment policies of each of the major institutions. But your own research (see Chapter 7) will give you much more detail of their concerns and views on your company and sector.

Targeting a particular institution has to go beyond 'targeting the Pru because it is an insurance company and therefore has long-term obligations to meet policy-holder commitments'. The Pru manages many different funds, all of which may have different investment policies. And the Pru itself will have overall 'constant' investment policies, for example on types of ethical investment, as well as changing ones like a decision to go 20 per cent liquid for a period of time. (To uncover an institution's stance on ethical investment, you can look at the share registers of other companies who, like you, may have a stake in South Africa and see which institutions are not bothered by this. County Council pension funds, for example, can be expected to have a heavy political bias.)

Types of institution

Institutional investors are made up of pension fund managers, insurance companies, unit trusts groups and investment trusts. By far the largest of these groups is the pension fund managers (see Figure

2) who, in a 1985 survey of institutional ownership of UK equities, owned over 30 per cent of all UK equities. Next came the insurance companies with about 20 per cent, and then unit trusts and investment trusts with barely ten per cent between them.

The remaining 40 per cent of shareholdings are by individuals (around 20 per cent), Government, charities (like the Church Commissioners, which is a huge investment institution), banks, other companies and overseas investors.

Over the post-war period, the institutions have come to control an increasing proportion of UK equity, partly because of the economies of scale in investment management, but also because of the tax incentive for investors to channel their investments in these forms. Around 7,000 people (even since 'Black Monday') are employed in the management of all this money.

How they work

As well as the simple breakdown of 'types' of institution, you must also remember that conglomerate funds, like those of the Pru, have their own long-term insurance funds to invest, but also have unit trusts whose objectives may vary from providing investors with income to capital growth and may seek to achieve these objectives by investing in specialist areas, either by industry (eg, 'high-tech'), geographically (eg, 'Japan Trust'), ethically, or through index-linking; it may also have fund management groups which manage other people's funds.

Pension funds and insurance funds are by far the most important of the institutions. Pension funds tend to be either self-managed or managed by one or more management groups. Overall investment policy is set by the trustees and should be fairly long-term to meet long-term obligations to pensioners. (They are, however, tempted by short-term opportunities and companies which complain about the City's preoccupation with short-termism should turn the spotlight on their own pension fund managers first.) Insurance companies, too, fall into two main categories: the life funds, whose investment horizons are long-term; and the general funds, which vary enormously in their outlooks.

On the subject of institutional long-term investment versus institutional inertia, David Walker, executive director at the Bank of England, once pointed out that: 'If "long-termism" amongst institutional investors means that they neither reduce their holdings nor indicate in any other way to their boards their concerns about a company of which they are members, it is not clear how such "long-termism" differs from inertia.

'With the benefit of hindsight, it is not difficult to call to mind situations in the last few years where a shorter-term approach, equival-

Institutional ownership of UK equities

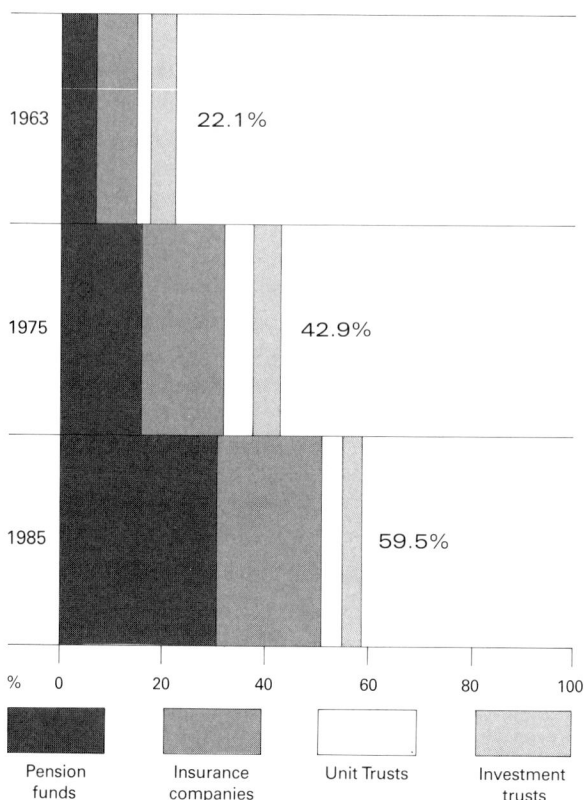

Year	Value
1963	22.1%
1975	42.9%
1985	59.5%

Pension funds · Insurance companies · Unit Trusts · Investment trusts

Source: CSO Financial Statistics; CSO 'The Ownership of Company Shares' – a Survey for 1985

Figure 2

ent to less patience, not to say less passivity, on the part of institutional shareholders might, with advantage, have been adopted at a much earlier stage.'

Getting to know the internal structure (as well as the investment policy) of the institutions is important for targeting purposes. Obviously, all have their tier of very senior people deciding the overall policy for all the group's investments, but the variety of structure beyond that is enormous.

In essence, however, there tend to be two main types of structure. In the first, fund managers manage almost entirely autonomously – for example, the fund manager of an income fund may have total discretion over which sectors, companies, even countries, he invests in so long as the investments are aimed at generating consistent income or growth. Because he manages a fund, he is, not unnaturally, given the title 'fund manager'. However, the fund managed may be quite small and the manager quite junior.

The second kind of structure has people at the top deciding allocations between, for instance, US property, Venezualan equity and Japanese gilts. Beneath them are people responsible for each of those areas; and, below them again, may be a team of people who specialize by industry sectors, making investment decisions based on outside research matched with their own opinions; or the team may comprise fewer managers who are assisted by internal analysts doing research.

The permutations of these structures is infinite. The term 'fund manager' can cover anything from a junior person managing a small fund, to a very senior person managing a range of huge funds. But it is a key part of the IR role to uncover them, and the names of the main individuals of the institutions being targeted. Also, it is imperative to find out, in advance of planning the IR programme, what influence outside analysts and fund management groups have on the institution being targeted.

Understanding the investment policy of each institution to be targeted is important not only to see if it should or could be an investor in the company but also for you to understand that if it suddenly sells half its holding in your company it may be to do with that policy – eg, shifting from one sector into another, or out of one national market into another, or maybe out of equities into an instrument like gilts – and nothing to do with the company itself. In the IR process, it is as important to discount investor activity as it is to credit it to the IR programme.

Growing specialists – third-party fund managers

The main fund management groups fall into two categories: the brokers and merchant banks which have fund management arms; and the fund management specialists, some of whom have sprung out of the merchant banks (like Mercury Asset Management) and some separate companies like Gartmore Investment Management and Ivory and Sime.

These are an increasingly influential and fast-growing groups and it would be a mistake to ignore them simply to concentrate on institutional investors and brokers. Again their structures can vary considerably, as can their level of investment control and influence.

It can also be difficult to keep track of their links with shareholding institutions, since their names often do not appear at any level of the nominee ladder. *Crawfords*, newspaper articles, etc, reveal many of the client/manager links, but there is no complete alternative to direct questions when you meet your shareholders, and advice from brokers.

Brokers – the 'middlemen'

As we said in Chapter 1, deregulation of the Stock Market completely changed the scene. Dual capacity led to fantastic expectations, huge staff turnover, telephone number salaries, an influx of Porsches, and an expectation from directors that trading profits would compensate them for shelling out those high salaries and sports cars. It also changed the entry route into brokers' houses and improved the equality of opportunity if not, yet, the quality of service.

The internal structure of the typical broker will include a research department, laid wall-to-wall with analysts usually covering one particular sector or two or three smaller ones each. Each is equipped with a huge variety of information sources. They are often very young with backgrounds varying from degrees in economics, business or underwater basketweaving, to former trade journalists. Some, though not many, will have come out of the sectors they are now covering and a few will still be of the old guard. There is, however, a noticeable trend towards employing people straight from university with *no* experience of industry whatsoever.

Other departments include the sales department, which can be as small as six to eight individuals, even in some of the large investment houses, or up to dozens in others; and the market-makers, fulfilling what used to be the old jobbers' role. Perhaps surprisingly, many of today's successful market-makers are ex-jobbers, now totally screen-based rather than trading from the Stock Exchange floor. They will be trading either on behalf of their own house, or for others. Some brokers will have a fund management group with a very large Chinese wall around – which may or may not be leaky. The corporate finance department will offer advice on markets, deals and regulatory matters for its own clients.

Traditionally, these were all separate roles but while Big Bang, and subsequent developments, have caused numerous changes to all of them, the change in the role of the broker's analyst has had the most impact on the role of IR.

Largely prompted by the telephone number salaries and Porsches, and the consequent demand by their employers for more and more out of the analysts, some have become deeply involved in market-making, equity sales and corporate finance.

As a result, many fund managers at the institutions can no longer be sure that they are receiving properly objective advice and that the analyst isn't trying, for example, to unload his own firm's position in a stock; or simply to generate trading volume (and so commission) to compensate for the massive drop in commission levels since Big Bang.

It is little wonder, then, that it has become quite routine for fund managers to criticize brokers' research publicly and stridently. From the IR manager's point-of-view, these changes in the role of the brokers' analyst have called for a major change in the part they play in the IR process (which is discussed in Chapter 5), but note that the loss of credibility of many analysts has, if anything, increased the influence of those who have retained the confidence of fund managers.

The financial media

Financial journalists are unquestionably a strong influence on investment decisions, as providers of both information and opinion.

The BPRI (Business Planning and Research International) research undertaken for this book listed 'press comment' as the second single most important source of information on investment in UK companies in the opinion of fund managers and brokers interviewed, second only to personal meetings with company management.

Because journalists tend to move frequently between jobs however, it can help to employ a firm of public relations consultants to keep track of them and to help set up interviews with the relevant ones. A relationship which has been built up over the years between a journalist and the PR consultant can also help to get a journalist to focus his attention on a particular company, if he knows that the consultant is now representing it.

Competition between companies for favourable media attention in the financial columns of the national dailies and Sundays – as well as in the management and business publications – is fierce: as any journalist will tell you, each day they are besieged with press releases and invitations to this press conference or to that lunch. Careful targeting of the right stories to the right financial journalist is therefore an essential part of segmentation in the IR process.

One important development over recent months has been the increasing number of broadcast media business programmes which have sprung up on the different channels – not to mention the advent of Sky and BSB. Programmes like *Business Daily*, *The Business Programme*, and *City Weekly* now supplement traditional favourites like *The Money Programme* and *Financial World Tonight* as important media through which companies can transmit their IR messages, and should not be ignored. As a final thought in this area, remember that financial journalists have enormous influence over investors, so that if PR and IR are totally separated, careful co-ordination will be crucial. It may well make more sense for financial journalists to be the clear responsibility of the IR staff.

Government departments

Particularly in takeover and merger situations, government bodies or departments, like the Office of Fair Trading (OFT) and the DTI, will become a key audience for the IR programme. It makes sense to have an understanding of how the OFT operates, the information it will require and how best to present it, long before you present the company's latest merger scheme.

Similarly, it helps to have 'friends' within the relevant government departments, and MPs on relevant industry committees who are kept up to date with the company's plans so that they can talk about you from a base of knowledge and confidence should their support ever be required.

The recent GEC-Siemens bid for Plessey – with its lengthy negotiations with the OFT, MOD, Home Office and DTI – shows that IR cannot be entirely divorced from the other communication disciplines.

CHAPTER 4

Packaging, promotion or pragmatism?
– *designing the message*

'We have decided to publish additional supplementary information that we think will help you measure both business value and managerial performance . . . We will attempt to lump major business activities in ways that aid analysis but do not swamp you with detail . . . Our goal is to give you important information in a form that we would wish to get it if our roles were reversed . . . However, we want to emphasize that our new presentation does not fall within the purview of our auditors, who in no way bless it. (In fact, they may be horrified; I don't want to ask.)' (Our friend Warren E Buffet, explaining Berkshire Hathaway Inc.'s 1988 report.)

'I have decided apparently, to show just two business sectors: bits and pieces'. (*Financial Times* Lex Column, comment on Hanson Trust's 1987 results.)

These extracts are a stark reminder of the difference in approach which can exist between organizations – not only in financial results, but also in statements of managerial strategy and almost all other fields of information-giving.

Quite simply, some companies willingly explain their plans to shareholders while others do not – and many are eventually forced from the first camp into the second when their earlier arrogance comes home to haunt them at moments of crisis.

Sadly, many companies who decide to turn over a new leaf and start to communicate more actively, do so half-heartedly and unprofessionally. They publish much longer annual reports and give twice as many presentations to investor groups, but they still say what they want to say rather than discuss what investors need to hear. As our friend Mr Buffet puts it: 'After all, any manager of a subsidiary company would find himself in hot water if he reported barebones GAAP [mandatory] numbers that omitted key information needed by his boss, the parent corporation's CEO. Why, then, should the CEO himself withold information vital to *his* bosses – the shareholder-owners of the corporation?'

If you were trying to sell a Rolls-Royce, you would not spend long on the subject of economy. A potential Volvo buyer, on the other hand, is rarely looking for high performance. Chapter 3 described the segmentation of the audience and our concern here must be the relevance of IR messages to each part of that audience.

All too often, companies fail to research, understand and address investors' concerns. Their communication then becomes ineffective or – worse – counter-productive.

This may be because the CEO cynically sees IR as a means of dressing up reality in the first place – he has no intention of really explaining his actions, but simply hopes the pretence of doing so will win some points. Like many before, he will usually reap just desserts!

Or it may be because the CEO has delegated the IR role too far down the organization chart. The poor individual is doing his best to keep investors informed, but is not in a position to know all the facts; the board's actions do not square with his explanations and concerns or suspicions mount.

Thus, the IR manager hears the CEO talk about commitment to growth and, knowing that the current fad in investment circles is earnings per share, commits the company to EPS growth. He wasn't to know that the CEO planned to take over the main player in the faster-growing sector of the market; but, since the target has a higher multiple than their own, EPS is about to be diluted. The CEO either has to disassociate him from the IR message – which will destroy the company's credibility – or change the strategy!

Or it may be because the IR manager is simply not sufficiently attuned to the market. He (and the CEO) mean well but, through lack of research, consideration or forward planning, they present messages which do not meet – or even run counter to – current investor concerns.

For example, BTR must have been profoundly shocked by its failure to capture Pilkington – a company whose performance had been lagging and which would probably have contributed more to BTR than it had to its original owners. BTR's wide search for a senior IR manager shortly afterwards can presumably be taken as indicating its acceptance that a good IR person would have been able to give warnings of the sudden shift in City fashion away from megabids and towards encumbent managements – as long as the latter were prepared to explain themselves fully.

The customer is always right

Your own research (see Chapter 11) should provide a good idea of the specific concerns and attractions for your own company that are affecting shareholder attitudes.

So if your research shows that investors know that 25 per cent of your revenue is earned outside your home country, but they wrongly think Africa is still the main contributor, this may well be affecting the company's valuation (African revenues are generally classed as low-quality earnings because of the political and currency risks). The IR objectives for the year might, therefore, include addressing this concern: clarify the actual proportions and then, as far as Africa is concerned, either find a way of publicizing your recent withdrawal or emphasize your excellent links with the governments concerned and your track record of never having your dividends blocked.

If surveys show that you are seen as constantly 'dribbling out' shares, maybe you should suggest that loan notes be used for some of the small acquisitions (they are equally tax-efficient for the seller) and then stop announcing them all (see Chapter 5 for mandatory announcements). On the other hand, if you are seen as too conservative – not taking advantage of expansion opportunities – perhaps you should be making more of research expenditure or equipment-upgrading programmes and encouraging the board to consider acquisitions.

General views – hardy favourites

Specific concerns about your company may dictate the most immediate communication, but there are key criteria which crop up in every survey of fund managers and which are ignored surprisingly often in company IR programmes. The weight given to them by different investors and at different times may vary, but the list itself is remarkably stable and should be the IR manager's bible of relevance (see Figure 3).

First on the list, almost invariably, is quality of management. A sparkling performance record and a fast-growing sector might mean very little if a new CEO has just moved in – he might ruin the first and move the company out of the second. Or, at the other extreme, take WPP, a dowdy supplier of supermarket trolleys: its performance record and sector became irrelevant as soon as Martin Sorrell moved in from Saatchi – within two years it has taken over two of the world's top ten ad agencies!

EVALUATION OF A COMPANY
Question: What are the major factors you take into account when making an overall assessment of a company?

EVALUATION OF MANAGEMENT
Question: How do you judge a company's management? What else would you take into account?

Evaluation of a company	Investors	Analysts
Quality/strength of management	89	69
Financial status, balance sheet strength, cashflow return on capital	58	32
Market they operate in	52	35
Track record, financial record	40	31
Earnings per share/prospective earnings	27	18
Position in market	20	15
Growth prospects	20	16
Future prospects	18	19
Profitability	17	15
Dividend growth/yield	16	9
Range of products/activities	16	9

Evaluation of management	Investors	Analysts
Track/past record	53	38
Personalities, meetings	53	43
Strategic planning	21	20
Communications, openness and frankness	17	16
Financial record	12	10
Perceived image in the market	12	3
Understanding their business	10	6
Performance of company	9	11
Quality of results	8	12
Ability to meet published targets	7	4
Responsiveness to shareholders	6	1
Experience	6	4
Clear direction	5	4
Achievements	5	6

Mori's report of a 1988 survey of UK institutional investors (147) and investment analysts (385) produced some useful general guidance for IR officers on, amongst other things, the criteria fund managers use to assess companies and to evaluate their managements.

Figure 3

But management quality does not necessarily mean simply the chief executive. Indeed, heavy PR for the CEO frequently leads to disaffection because it implies a lack of supporting managers (think about Richard Branson of Virgin or Michael Ashcroft of ADT) or raises fears about succession (eg, Owen Green or Hanson/White).

Management quality – teamwork wins

At the end of the day, successful companies need strong leadership and good management teamwork – and investors know it. Their ideal will be a competent, highly-committed CEO (which suggests one who has little time for self-publicity, though not necessarily a hermit) with a good surrounding team.

Down with politicians

One very senior fund manager recently stated a very simple measurement system. He said he awards a company one mark for each non-executive on the board, one for each director promoted from within and one for each with marketing or operations experience in the company's sector. Then he deducts a mark for each accountant, peer or MP. He says very few UK companies get positive marks.

In IR terms, then, it will be important to show the degree to which your company meets this ideal. Asked how they judge a company's management, fund managers list track record, personality/meetings and strategic planning/clear direction amongst other criteria.

Clearly, it will help to point to the past record of each member of the team, but it will also be important for investors to stare into their steely blue eyes and judge for themselves. A CEO who is excellent at small-talk but superficial, evasive or ignorant about the business, and yet never allows his line managers to accompany him, is probably the worst combination.

Yet, investors do not expect all the managers to be slick, outgoing geniuses. Again, relevance is the key: the production director is probably crucial in a heavy manufacturer; the marketing or design directors in a consumer electronics outfit; maybe the distribution director in a retail firm. In service companies, it might be important to judge depth of management, whereas the small team of strategic planners might be the key in a pure conglomerate.

They're not just pretty faces

But fund managers will be looking for more than a team of workaholics. They want to know what the team's plans are and how collectively committed the directors are to them.

This can be a highly dangerous area – particularly in the fast-moving company or industry. Obviously, the team will not wish to give away its plans for leaving the opposition behind, since the fund manager is sure to want the opposition's reaction – which would involve telling him the plan. Yet, a superficial 'we aim to be the best . . . in Europe' is unlikely to be convincing on its own.

Furthermore, investors are not usually as impressed by financial objectives ('we are determined to improve shareholder value') as they are by obviously well-thought-out and attainable industrial strategies ('we intend to consolidate our market leadership in the UK this year and expand it into France over the next two years').

Companies are almost universally condemned for saying too little about their strategies and prospects in their IR messages. Most funds *do* have long-term objectives and they want to know if yours will satisfy theirs.

Window dressing – performance ratios

The second key investment criterion almost invariably involves the company's performance, and here too relevance is the main factor. General investment trends vary according to fashion, economic cycle, etc, (see Which way is the wind blowing, page 62) but there are time-honoured measures which must be properly understood and assessed.

As we have already argued, there is little point in promoting your shares as a high-yield investment to a capital growth fund or as cash-generative to a fan of gearing ratios.

It is not a case of seeking your most favourable ratio and then promoting that and suppressing all other figures. Most intelligent fund managers will want to assess you on several criteria, and will probably assume the worst if you try to prevent them from reaching the figures relevant to them. Window-dressing, then, will usually be recognized and condemned.

However, intelligent arguments as to why one ratio is more relevant than another in your case will often be accepted (eventually) – as long as *both* ratios are given.

The first golden rule is to stay one step ahead. Make sure you have compared yourself with what investors see as your peer group, on *all* of the ratios. Since this is what the market will do (at least between them, even if each investor only looks at a few), you might as well have your arguments prepared and rehearsed.

If your gearing is high, don't try to hide it, but explain *why* interest cover is more relevant. If your cashflow is weak, explain that R&D spend is high and then point to the research-to-launch ratio to show your potential.

If you can't beat 'em, join 'em

After several years of pointing out the irrelevance of gearing in measuring its financial strength (because its acquisitions of asset-poor but cash-generative service companies reduced its equity through goodwill write-offs *and* increased its borrowings) and pointing, with limited success, to its high interest cover, BET decided to swim with the tide. It gained shareholder approval to issue variable-dividend preference shares in the USA. These have many of the characteristics of debt but are, legally, perpetual equity, so they reduced the company's gearing without diluting its earnings.

The preference shares are not universally viewed as equity but they allow the company to argue that if preference shares are debt, goodwill should be added back to equity. Interest cover is now being more widely accepted as a better measure of financial strength than gearing for service companies.

If you cannot explain a poor ratio, ask the accountants to do so – either they will have a sensible answer or you have found a problem the CEO should look into, before the market does.

Note that we suggest looking at the ratios *relative to your peer group*. We'll return to this theme in Chapter 11 but it's relevant here, too. If you are responsible for IR in a true industry leader, you may very well find yourself arguing, on behalf of the whole industry, that this ratio is more relevant than that and that your sector is undervalued because of investors' misunderstanding of this factor.

Most IR managers, however, will find themselves primarily asked to compete with other similar companies. It may be that the investment manager at ABC pension fund will decide to switch from electronics to property, but most fund managers will be choosing between GEC, Siemens and Texas Instruments – or even between GEC, Racal and Plessey (if they all survive).

They will be looking at brokers' reports, datastream charts, Extel cards, Topic screens, IBES tables, etc, and asking you why your price/earnings, return on equity, price to book or cashflow ratios are lower than those of your peer group. All of these services are available and you should monitor their output. If you cannot justify the cost of your own subscription to any or all of them, your broker will usually be willing to send you a regular copy or print-out. Going into battle with investors without prior study of their information sources is like stepping into a boxing ring with the heavyweight champion without checking which hand he leads with!

Remember, too, that different performance ratios will be important to different investors – so be prepared. Chapter 3 distinguishes between income-orientated and capital growth funds, trading-orientated analysts and long-term individuals. Chapters 7–10 point out that foreign investors are likely to focus on another factor again. The guideline must be to put yourself in the audience's shoes and try to imagine which measures of performance you would focus on, in which order and relative to whom.

Which way is the wind blowing?

But investment criteria also vary over time. Economic cycles, fashion, press comment, political change and many other factors can cause widespread changes in general priorities.

Once again, anticipation can pay high dividends when circumstances change inside the company or in the sector or market at large. The IR manager that could anticipate the economic or political change before the market would be worth his weight in platinum. But a competent IR manager should be able to anticipate *likely* questions from investors once the change has taken place, and prepare the answers. He may be powerless to prevent the crash but should be able to limit excessive damage to the company by recognizing that priorities have changed and giving an assessment of the effect.

When UK monetary policy was tightened in late 1988, the retail sector, not surprisingly, nose-dived as investors anticipated a slowdown in consumer spending. But some retailers' shares suffered more than others – as a result of both real and imaginary concerns. A secondary effect followed soon afterwards which should have been predictable – distribution companies came under the spotlight. Yet NFC, which had recently used several famous retailers as examples of its customers when launching its share listing, was given wide praise for having anticipated investors' questions, while some competitors were caught embarrassingly unprepared – unable to answer questions about the proportion of their revenues earned from retailers.

Similarly, the slowdown in UK housebuilding showed up huge differences in IR skills amongst the construction companies and their suppliers: some were well-prepared with statistics on their forward order books from other construction sectors; others tried to make the same points but without facts and figures – and the market's reaction served them right. It's worth bearing in mind that analysts depend on companies for much of their information and will be seeking sector as well as company data.

Relevance and flexibility

In summary, then, designing IR messages must be a case of selection and emphasis, not seclusion and deceit.

Most of the facts will be important to someone, but each segment of the audience will have different priorities. None of them will thank you for directing too much irrelevant information at them, but all of them will be suspicious – and, eventually, hostile – if you conceal what they want to know.

Any FD can hide embarrassing information for a period of time but such deception has a habit of surfacing in the end. As good old Warren E Buffet puts it: 'CEOs are free to treat [accounting requirement] as a beginning rather than an end to their obligations to inform owners and creditors – and indeed they should.'

Or, closer to home, the chairman of London's Stock Exchange said recently: 'It is notable that the companies that complain about short-termism in the City are generally those which have done least to keep their shareholders properly informed. These are the companies which do not earn – and are unlikely to gain – their shareholders' loyalty and support'.

PART II

EXECUTING
THE
PROGRAMME

CHAPTER 5

Is it all City lunches?
– day-to-day IR techniques and methods

'We had ABC plc in today. It's not general knowledge but they're about to sign a massive deal in Turkey. We're upping our forecast by 20 per cent. How many shares shall I put you down for?'

This kind of conversation is largely a thing of the past as regulations tighten and court cases increase. So what has replaced it? Not so many years ago it really was all City lunches. More was probably spent on City lunches than on sweeping the factory floor; and more on sweeping the factory floor than on all other forms of corporate communications added together.

However, as companies are waking up to the fact that they actually need to market their shares and, therefore, need to keep investors and their advisors better informed, so the techniques for passing on such information are becoming more varied and practical. So, having designed the messages, what are your main vehicles for delivering them?

The main channels of 'peace time' communication are:

- the annual report and accounts
- the interim report
- company fact books
- databases and directories
- advertising
- company announcements
- meetings and presentations
- AGMs and shareholder meetings.

The annual report and accounts

A good example of a company which has reassessed the role of its annual report in the marketing mix is, perhaps incredibly, the BBC. Not content with the profits to be made from its BBC Enterprises offshoot, it began 1988 with a TV campaign promoting its new-style annual report (replacing the old BBC Handbook) – a two-hour programme on the company, and a 24-page supplement for *Radio Times* readers.

By the end of the first week of the New Year, it had sold out of copies of the annual report; the *Radio Times* with the insert sold in record fast time; and its programme on BBC TV and radio personalities and programme-makers at work did surprisingly well in the ratings.

How this kind of merchandising goes down with shareholders is perhaps a moot point (particularly for the BBC which has no shareholders in the traditional sense). A fine balance has to be maintained between investing in a prestigious and attractive annual report and showing investors that their money is being spent wisely. The annual report, first and foremost, is a vehicle for conveying information to shareholders. Its marketing role, if it has one at all, should be secondary.

With that in mind, a fine balance also needs to be struck between information which conveys the company's status accurately, and that which points towards unattainable expectations.

One of the biggest danger areas here is the 'mission statement'. While the company's strategy is a key criterion for investment decisions, attempting to package the strategy into an all-embracing mission statement can easily become a hostage to fortune – a load of public relations hype to which the management can't possibly relate. And if the managers let it be known that that's all it is, they blow the credibility of the entire annual report – if they'll let someone print a mission statement they do not believe in at the front of their report, why should they prevent any other illusory or exaggerated material appearing in the rest of the book?

Achievement of strategic goals can take years to accomplish and while the company's management may know what those goals are over the long term, to let the cat out of the bag too early may put the company under unwanted pressure, as well as giving the game away to competitors.

An all-embracing strategy, summed-up in a mission statement, that is clearly not being attained will make the company's management look weak. In these cases it should be replaced by a good description of the businesses in which the company is involved, and the review section should give as good an idea as possible of where the company is going.

The chairman's statement should ideally tell the shareholders what they need to hear – the good news as well as the bad – and not what the chairman wants to say. That should be its guiding principle and the IR manager should challenge the chairman, if necessary, to ensure that shareholders' requirements are being adequately addressed. And if he is over-ruled, an attempt should be made to redress the balance somewhere else in the report – perhaps the chief executive will be less intransigent with his review.

The purpose of the chairman's statement is to summarize the results of the year, and to restate the company's strategic objectives and priorities. It may talk, in general terms, about trading prospects for the company but the chairman should think carefully before saying anything that might be interpreted as a forecast. Should the company, later in the year, find itself on either end of an acquisition then the chairman may be forced by the Stock Exchange to publish an audited forecast which, otherwise, might not have been necessary. And the Stock Exchange will not allow the chairman to make forecasts only in good years.

The 'personality' of the annual report

The annual report provides the main benchmark for investors and analysts to judge a company's performance and culture. It is no longer sufficient to provide shareholders with bare facts as they are legally bound to, dressed up with pretty graphics and often incomprehensible figures. But the style of the annual report will often reflect the importance that is attached to communications by the chairman or chief executive.

It takes an aggressive chairman, such as Sir Christopher Hogg of Courtaulds, to launch a £1m new corporate identity simultaneously with the company's annual report. The new image ran right through the report and gave some indication of the way the company hoped to use it in the future. The new report was intended to show the company's intention to compete more aggressively overseas and to incentivize its workforce.

The report, published in 1987, was used to show that the chairman's long-term business objectives, first reported four years previously, had boosted growth and earnings. The message was just as important for employees:

'The momentum for change and improvement will be boosted by the many changes we have been making to bring on new and younger managers and to release resources at the top to the group's development and expansion,' said the statement. 'Courtaulds now has real strength where it matters most – in its people.'

The executive review

This needs to describe the relative successes of each of the principal trading divisions – as distinct from the directors' report which, under Companies Act requirements, has to cover the 'motherhood' items, such as donations to charities, the company's policy as an equal opportunities employer and so on. (Detailed items for disclosure are to be found in the Stock Exchange's Yellow Book, and in the General Undertaking for USM companies.)

There is a trend nowadays to combine the directors' report with the executive review. This means that since the directors' report is subject to review by the auditors, so is the executive review – which is probably no bad thing since it encourages the review to err on the side of fact. And combining the two can make it easier for the investor to get an overall picture of the company in one, uninterrupted, reading.

The Stock Exchange recommends that companies should make the most of the communications opportunity provided by the annual report to reinforce their corporate message in simple and non-technical terms; and to highlight key facts, not only about the business but also about key personnel. Many companies seem to interpret this advice as a requirement for many more photographs and graphs which is fine so long as they are used for clarification and not for jollification.

Whichever way it is done, the annual report should be designed to give private shareholders an annual opportunity to assess the potential of their investment. Private investors do not see the constant analysis and comparative measurement that the fund managers see, and rely heavily on this document. A report of events in the year under review has some value, but they need to know where the company is going – what the managers are trying to do and what this means to the value of the IR investment. They need to know what the dividend policy is and how the company is investing for the future – in terms of research and training, for instance.

They also need to know how the company is managed and what its values and liabilities are, plus an explanation of the business to be transacted at the AGM.

In the USA, a heavily-regulated annual document – form 20F – is required by the regulatory authorities. There may be much to be said for introducing some elements of this reporting requirement throughout Europe, since it must include a description of the business and a form of disclosure of its results (the 'Management discussion and analysis of results from continuing operations') for which the directors are legally responsible. Any company which reports under these requirements is only too aware of how much more information it exposes.

When it comes to the figures section of the report, much controversy is raging at present over the 'loss of identity' of the balance sheet. The problem is that UK balance sheets contain a mixture of costs and valuations (the current example being brand valuations). The costs mean little, since they are often costs incurred at different times which have been added together. Valuations can be done on a number of different bases, none of which are compatible. Also, balance sheets often do not show liabilities which should be there (a practice known as 'off balance sheet finance').

This is all significant because balance sheets are one of the prime sources of financial information about a company, and therefore important to the efficient running of financial markets. Investors, analysts and financial journalists use balance sheet-based indicators when making judgments about companies: gearing, net assets and return on capital. As a result, the consumers of capital, the companies, are forced to pay close attention to the presentation of their balance sheets to the financial markets.

A large part of the problem is that accountants cannot decide what balance sheets are for. There are two opposing views. On the one hand there are those who say they should simply be a record of money which a company has spent. The other view is that they should (and to an extent do) give an indication of value – though not a company's full value, since only the Stock Market can arrive at this figure.

The value argument makes traditional accountants extremely angry because they believe balance sheets should stick to showing costs (which are measurable, therefore precise) rather than values (which are subjective and therefore largely meaningless). If not, they become worthless.

The Institute of Chartered Accountants of Scotland has argued, however, that balance sheets should record values because: 'Business activity is about the adding of value, so financial statements should reflect this'.

The argument is clearly set to run and run. In the meantime, it remains open season for companies who want to present their accounts in the best light. IR managers obviously have to work out with the CEO and FD what stance their own company is going to take and explain its reasons for doing so as clearly as possible.

The *interim report* provides a half-yearly opportunity to bring investors up-to-date with the company's progress and to make comparisons with its profit or loss for the corresponding six months of the previous year. The report can either be sent to the holders of all listed securities, or published as a paid advertisement in two national daily newspapers (only one in the case of companies traded on the USM). Very few companies nowadays take the second option; indeed, most include more information than is mandatory and some companies – particularly those listed in the USA – produce quarterly reports although they are no longer obliged to do so. Similarly, balance sheet figures are not required for UK interim reports, but any company seeking international shareholders will need to give at least some balance sheet data. As well as sending the annual and interim reports to shareholders, they should also be sent to the company's core list of fund managers and analysts.

UK requirement for foreign companies

Foreign companies listed in the UK must circulate an English language annual report and accounts, plus an auditor's report, for their 12-month period. Foreign companies do not have to comply with UK accounting standards but should conform to those of the International Accounting Standard Committee. US auditor's reports are acceptable. Statements of the interests of directors and their families, and of each holder of five per cent or more of the share capital, or of options for this amount, must be included. The accounts must state that no pre-emptive rights exist and provide information for shareholders' tax relief. Companies with bearer shareholders must put an announcement in two daily papers published in the UK stating where and when free copies of reports and accounts in written English can be obtained.

Company fact books

Background information on the company and the industry in which it operates which is not available in the annual report or other forms of corporate literature can be usefully packaged in a fact book aimed at fund managers and analysts. This is also a useful vehicle for the company's management who have to deal with analysts, and can usefully be sent with a welcoming letter to all new shareholders, provided it is not *too* turgid.

You must be aware of what the intended recipients really want. There is no point in reproducing, for the sake of it, industry data which is easily accessible elsewhere. However, it can be helpful to analysts and others if the company has taken the trouble to pull together published data which is not available from a single source or which is not available from anyone else.

Considerable care is needed to balance conflicting requirements. If the book is too comprehensive it may leave little for analysts to add and hence discourage them from publishing research reports; it may give away commercially-sensitive information; or it may become wholly indigestible. If it is too superficial, it may be helpful only to private shareholders.

There are alternative approaches which can be more acceptable in some cases. Carefully briefing a good analyst can result in a reference book with more credibility. However, it can be argued that, even if no single fact is price-sensitive, the collection of facts *is*, and giving one analyst exclusive access to it is breaking the spirit, and possibly the letter, of the rules.

Some publishers are prepared to research and write such reports on companies, often publishing them as paid-for supplements with run-on copies available for the company to buy and distribute. (*Institutional Investor*, *Euromoney*, and the *Financial Times*, for instance, offer this service. Extel publishes glossy, company-produced supplements to its famous Extel cards and many other information companies have variations on this theme.)

Companies listed in the USA can often use their form 20F (see page 70) as a fact book, with its legal status pointed out to add credibility. But the companies who avoid *any* distribution of their 20F, and publish glossy fact books, raise some suspicion about their willingness to be honest and open!

Databases and directories

The last ten years, in particular, have seen a proliferation of sources of information used by investors and their advisers. These are often enormously useful to the IR manager, not only as a means of communication but also for keeping himself informed.

The most obvious in the UK is TOPIC, the Stock Exchange screen-based information source used by most professionals. IR managers not able to watch their company's share price and volume moving are not going to be fully in tune with the people ringing them. Prestel and Teletext are cheaper, but their information is inadequate and they are not constantly updated. More expensive than TOPIC, Reuters 'Equity 2000' has all of the key TOPIC information, a layout you can design yourself and, of course, the Reuters news services. So you can design a screen to show you the FT index and your own shares (price, volume, change during the day, etc) plus several competitive shares and the latest City news.

Databases and directories are key communication media. They display company news and your announcements need to be written with your audience in mind. More recently, another screen-based information service widely used by professionals, First Call, has introduced a service allowing companies to display information and news. Like well-used directories, this might be a useful supplement to your efforts. Remember, however, that a junior functionary handling your entries in directories and databases may not be up-to-date on IR objectives.

Telephone enquiry lines

A useful new service you can establish for your shareholders, which can also give you an opportunity to collect their views and communicate with them, is a telephone enquiry line. The *Financial Times* and Telephone Information Services both offer a variety of services ranging from a recorded message from you which plays after a market report and your current share price (you can change the message several times) to a series of links into more complex information, or even a link to your own enquiry line, manned by the telephone marketing company.

The services use a separate number for each company but are administered by the supplier and statistics indicate that they are popular with investors. Certainly they are a relatively simple way of distributing your basic message and news independently of the Press and electronic media. The ultimate, of course, is your own 0800 telephone number follow-on, allowing two-way communication between you and your shareholders.

Advertising

It is probably in the area of financial advertising that shareholders become most sensitive about where promotional funds are being spent. Fund managers, too, are often cynical about financial advertising because the need to do it in the first place indicates a failure in the IR programme!

However, there is enough research around to show that advertising *does* positively influence the attitude of fund managers; as does advertising seen by fund managers but aimed at the company's customers, because it demonstrates the company's aggressive pursuit of its business strategy.

Paying to get your financial results in the national press through advertisements may be the only route open to some companies who are unable to attain editorial coverage for their performance. This will often be the case for USM-traded companies and smaller PLCs, and represents a sensible tactic to reach investors and draw attention from financial journalists.

Depending on what the financial results are, it can sometimes be a risky tactic for larger PLCs who are sure to be covered in the editorial columns. You could end up with your 'very pleased' advertisement sitting alongside a piece of editorial copy that says your only future hope of salvation is to be taken over. However, when all is said and done, advertising does provide a useful short-cut to presenting performance – and presenting it in *your* way – so long as it is just one of the communications firearms in your armoury; and that the message is kept clear and simple.

Why some companies use TV advertising

Hanson Trust was shocked to discover that private shareholders of the Imperial Group were against its proposed takeover bid. The shareholders didn't know who Hanson was but had a feeling it was a rapacious asset-stripper. So Hanson embarked on a major television advertising campaign.

ADT's sponsorship of the London Marathon was partly aimed at customers but also at consolidating its improving image with shareholders.

Research shows that BET's first ever television commercials – aimed at customers – were so widely seen by the financial community that it was able to drop the advertising of its financial results.

Company announcements

In summary, the four main rules laid down by the Stock Exchange on company disclosure (known as class 1–4) state that:

- Any transaction (usually acquisition or disposal) amounting to 15 per cent or more of the company's assets or profits requires full disclosure of information, including a shareholder circular and, in certain cases over 25 per cent, an extraordinary general meeting.
- Transactions amounting to five–15 per cent of the company's total assets or profits or *any* transaction involving the issue of the company's shares *must* be announced at least to the stock exchanges where the company is listed. Also, any transaction in which a director is involved must be announced.
- Smaller transactions which do not involve the issue of shares or the involvement of a director need not be announced at all. However, if *any* public announcement of the transaction is made, it *must* include the information in the point below and must be sent to the stock exchanges first.
- If any announcement of a transaction is to be made (see three points above), the regulations require the disclosure of *either* the

consideration to be paid or received, *or* the value of the assets to be acquired or divested.

The UK authorities used to be prepared to accept revenue or profit as an indication of size in lesser transactions, instead of assets or consideration. However, the Financial Services Act has caused a considerable tightening of regulation and more formal requirements. It is still useful to give either revenue or profit as well, since this is an inevitable question that will be asked; and the answer could be deemed price-sensitive if it has not been disclosed formally.

Where most of a company's acquisitions or disposals fall into the smaller category, the effects of the rules must be fully understood. Subsidiary companies need to give the parent listed company the maximum possible notice, with clear details of timing, strategic and operational factors, assets and consideration, as well as their own preference regarding announcement.

If a company does not wish to disclose the assets or consideration (where no shares have been involved) its only option is to make no public announcement.

The problem here is really twofold. The parent company may not wish to be seen by the financial community as making too many 'relatively insignificant' acquisitions or disposals, while, on the other hand, the subsidiary involved may want to make an announcement for good commercial and marketing reasons.

The best solution is to use your common sense. The subsidiary can brief a *few* individual trade magazine journalists, for example, but any collective briefing, a wide campaign of individual trade journal or local newspaper briefings, or *any* briefing of national or regional newspapers, could be deemed to be a public announcement.

Employee publications are also generally deemed to be 'public' but an internal memo (so long as it is not marked 'press release' or similar, and is not displayed in areas available to the public) is permissible.

In present circumstances (see Wider dissemination of information, page 13), getting the timing of announcements right is absolutely crucial. Anything involving class 1, 2 or 3 classification (summarized at the beginning of this section on company announcements) means that the Stock Exchange must receive the announcement first; and details of the announcement must have gone up on the Stock Exchange Topic screen before it is distributed to other groups.

Timing of the announcement can obviously be further complicated by press deadlines, particularly if you have to accommodate more than one time zone.

If the company is listed overseas, especially on one of the major exchanges such as New York, then every effort should be made to release the information simultaneously if you're really serious about your overseas IR programme.

Remember too that consideration needs to be given to having a board member available in the overseas capital(s) where the shares are listed to brief analysts and the Press and respond to questions. But, at the risk of stating the obvious (when it is apparently not so obvious to some) the number of questions arising will be greatly reduced if the announcement has anticipated most of them and has been written concisely.

Short-form reports

The Finance Act 1989 finally permitted the use of short-form annual reports by UK companies. These provide a useful means of supplementing the annual report, and a means of conveying complicated and tedious financial information to employees and private investors, particularly for companies with large numbers of private shareholders, or those involved in Personal Equity Plans (PEPs).Certainly, research abounds which shows which parts of the annual report are actually read by those not interested in the financial minutiae. Perhaps their only drawback is that they may require extensive re-writing from the original annual report. Once that has been done, they will need to be checked by the auditors and distributed (to shareholders).

Some view this as a means of reducing the information available to shareholders; but it need not be. The Department of Trade and Industry has proposed that companies write to all shareholders, pointing out the implications of the short-form accounts and giving them the option of receiving the full report. In addition, companies could publicize a 0800 telephone number and make the full accounts available by the next day. Regulations now demand such a lot of information in annual reports that they are largely incomprehensible to the private shareholder; a well-prepared short-form version will probably, therefore, get across *more* information rather than less.

Market feedback

Acting as the board's antennae on investment concerns and attitudes is an essential part of the IR role. Regular feedback of information can provide a helpful background for future decisions and the IR manager is, in many ways, better placed to pose unpopular or undiplomatic questions than other executives, because it is his job to anticipate investors' reactions.

Conversations with investors and intermediaries often signpost emerging concerns or trends, so notes of questions and answers should be taken at all important meetings and summaries of these, together with noted investor concerns, circulated regularly to the CEO and CFO. Such summaries also provide invaluable material for developing 'question and answer' rehearsal sessions for those participating in future company financial presentations.

More formal – and, perhaps, objective – summaries of attitudes should be sought from research surveys (see Chapter 11), consultants or house brokers on a regular basis. But there is no doubt that informal, constant feedback is a key benefit which the good IR manager can provide.

Brokers' lunches – should you feed each other?

With information, 'yes' is the short answer but not necessarily with nutritional sustenance at the same time. Although brokers' lunches have been largely discredited, meetings with brokers remain important for companies if they are to achieve fair coverage of their activities in brokers' circulars.

Brokers' *analysts*, involved in the 'sell side' of the brokers' operation should ideally be given full but collective briefings at least twice a year (at annual and interim results stage) and at other major events, such as a large acquisition. They may well want a private conversation afterwards but the briefing can get across the main points to the primary analysts much more efficiently.

If practicable, each analyst covering the company's sector should also be seen individually at least once a year, before the IR manager sees the figures, in order to help them put together brokers' reports to predict the full and half-year results.

Preferential treatment, in terms of the number of meetings and opportunities to meet operational and other senior management should be given only to those analysts who really demonstrate an interest in following the affairs of the company and in trying to understand it, and who have true influence on the company's shares (see Chapter 11).

So, while the IR manager must be prepared to see every analyst who wants to come in and talk, there should be no reason for them to meet with other members of the company's management unless they are amongst the more important ones (to the company *or* the market). However, this selectivity should only be practised if the company can fully justify it. If proper measurements of broker influence are constantly made, then it is quite fair to give some favourable treatment to the top analysts, but the company can easily open itself to accusations of favouring only the favourable analysts if it cannot demonstrate proper justification.

The IR manager must also exercise caution in volunteering

information. He certainly needn't volunteer any information at all if it is thought that the analyst is going to treat it superficially; the manager can restrict himself simply to answering questions. But caution is paramount if there appears to be a danger of volunteering price-sensitive information. Even an occasional 'nod and a wink' to indicate to the analyst that he is on the right track runs the risk of making the analyst an involuntary 'insider dealer'.

Particularly useful to analysts are facility visits where they see for themselves the operational end of the company and talk to line management (who will need briefing).

Facility visits are a relatively simple exercise for companies with only one line of business but more complicated for those in several different types of business. Either several facility visits need to be fixed up during the year or an exhibition or presentation of the company's different activities can be drawn together for analysts, investors and others to see the company 'at a glance'. In these cases, though, it is important that line managers from the various businesses are openly available and, while they should be briefed on what they are allowed to disclose, any effort to over-promote a 'company line' will usually be very obvious.

In between these formal events, lunches or dinners for key analysts to meet key managers informally may do a lot to help their view of your depth of management. It might also help your managers to understand the pressures on the head office.

Facility visits can go wrong!

On one famous occasion, a group of analysts had been invited to the North of England to visit a factory using the latest technology to glaze enamel. They were being flown from Gatwick, which unfortunately had become fog-bound, so delaying their arrival at the factory by a couple of hours.

As soon as they arrived inside the factory to see the glinting new technology in action, a loud whistle blew and everything promptly shut down as the workforce left for its lunch break.

This was in the days when unions were all-powerful, and the analysts were on a tight schedule, so the managing director had no alternative but to walk them round, explaining what they would be seeing if only everything was working.

He had just reached the end of the production line when a caretaker leapt to his feet, pressed a button and the entire works spluttered into life.

Beaming with pleasure, the MD mentally applauded the care-taker on the initiative he had shown on seeing his predicament and told the expectant analysts that, any moment now, they would witness enamel products coming through in a perfectly glazed state. As the door on the production line opened and they all gazed in anticipatory admiration, looks turned from disbelief to utter horror as a pork pie came bouncing through – perfectly heated for the caretaker's lunch!

The brokers' sales team, there to follow-up on the analysts' 'buy' recommendation, are often neglected by the IR manager. If the analysts recommend buying your stock but the institutional funds don't buy it, it may well be that the message is not getting through to, or is not inspiring, the sales team. It might then be worth arranging, once or twice a year, to give them an update on the company's activities and the opportunity to talk with line management. Remember that they'll be looking for anecdotal sales points, not a pure regurgitation of published facts and figures.

Fund managers – friend or foe?

They can be either, depending on their investment policies and the appropriateness of your business objectives to those policies. The importance of understanding the policies was described in Chapter 3, but of equal importance is to get a grasp on how each is structured so that – as with any marketing exercise – you know who you are trying to reach and how to reach them. Fund management groups increasingly employ their own buyside analysts as distrust of the objectivity and quality of brokers' analysts' information escalates.

Fund management group analysts may either cover a whole range of sectors or be sector or company specific; so don't rely on all of them having the same information. Additionally, because of the diversity of titles which fund management groups bestow on their employees you may think you're rushing into the City to meet a fund manager only to discover you are eye-to-eye with a very young analyst who has been accorded the grand title of fund manager.

Ideally, the company's top IR team, including at least one board member, should make a full presentation to middle-level and junior fund managers once a year, probably at the time of the preliminary results or at times of special significance (see next chapter). And these should include not only those based in London but also Edinburgh, Glasgow, and possibly provincial centres like Manchester and Birmingham.

Such meetings can be organized by the company's brokers (they will always argue that they should be the ones in charge) but, increasingly, institutions prefer meetings to be arranged by the companies direct – always provided that you know who are your top existing and non-shareholders. It may be sensible to ask your house broker for background information on the fund managers.

Middle-level and senior fund managers will also want to see members of your top team on occasions, apart from the annual presentation, which can cause time problems for senior management. So judgment and some degree of policing may need to be exercised to keep demands down to a reasonable level.

By and large, though, middle and senior level managers won't mind being mixed in groups to cut down some of the time involved. One helpful criterion to use here is that if the request is for a one-on-one meeting, then the fund manager in question should be seen by the IR manager accompanied perhaps by a board director if the fund is worth it; if groups of six to ten can be arranged, however, then it's worth involving either the CEO or the CFO.

Much IR work is reactive, but there should be a plan in place for meeting at least the top 50 institutional investors and perhaps the top 50 non-investors, again in groups of six to ten, on a regular basis – probably once every year or 18 months. If your segmentation system is up to it, it may be better to have two parallel series of lunches or dinners. The chairman and CEO can host regular meetings for a few top fund managers at a time (possibly with other VIP guests, since these are likely to be 'getting to know you' sessions, not investment seminars). And separately, the FD or another director can host a series of lunches or dinners with six to ten fund managers at a time, possibly preceded by a short presentation. Finally, a few of the huge funds will expect an exclusive meeting at least every other year. Of course, if the company wants its IR manager to stay in touch with investors, company strategy and management views – as well as to retain credibility with fund managers – it is important that he attends all of these meetings.

The AGM – legal bore or communication opportunity?

If direct communication with shareholders is hard to arrange, the AGM is an obvious opportunity – or is it? Different companies take different views here, and rightly so, because there is no universal answer. All depends on your objectives and style. The legal requirements of an AGM make it necessarily a formal occasion, unsuitable for some companies, and involving the whole board – which may or may not be a good thing, depending on the number and presentability of the non-executives. Furthermore, it provides a platform for aggressive questioning: for instance, if you are likely to have an anti-apartheid or environmental lobby there, you may not want to encourage shareholders to come! Illustrating the different approaches, United Biscuits has a film show and full lunch following its AGM in Edinburgh (with a variety of food from its own companies, vividly making the point that UB is more than a biscuit maker) while Burton takes interested shareholders on a guided tour of a shop. At the other extreme, BET leaves its AGM as a deliberately boring event and encourages shareholders to attend separate events.

The important thing is to approach the AGM like any other part of the IR programme – with proper planning. Decide whether or not you want it to be a communication exercise and plan it accordingly. Generally speaking, most shareholders will not come unless you encourage them to or there is serious dissent against the board's policies – in which case, it is usually obvious from letters and proxy cards.

Things can go wrong, of course. One of the most famous farces was Abbey National's meeting early in 1989 to approve its conversion to a PLC. At a cost of a reported £700,000 to stage, the meeting was held at the vast Wembley Arena with accommodation for 30,000 people. About 1,000 society members braved the pouring rain to attend. To make matters worse, the Society sustained its reputation for misjudging shareholder interest when 340 people did their best to fill the 6,000 capacity Alexandra Palace at its annual meeting on 26 April 1989. Yet both these situations were avoidable – why did the company not ask shareholders to indicate their intentions, with an inducement for them to do so (eg, a prize draw of reply cards)?

Shareholder meetings – AGM extension or bun-fight?

For those companies that decide the AGM is unsuitable for its IR purposes, shareholder meetings are the obvious alternative. But this phrase covers a multitude of possibilities. Some companies – BT, Shell, and ADT for example – use shareholder meetings more to take the AGM to (cheaper) regional venues, with their board (or some of it) still up on a formal dais and questions and answers handled formally and publicly. Others take a very different approach, with displays, entertainment and management available for private, informal contact. Racal's open days are a well-known example but they show that the company has plenty of choices, with research showing how much investors appreciate the effort.

Arranging this wide variety of meetings can create a lot of administrative hassle for the IR department or consultancy. The benefit is that the meetings make the company less dependent on its broker for investor contact: if you're in the position of handling them yourself, you can always ask the broker to add names or ask two or more brokers to organize presentations for 50 institutions and supplement your own list of invitees. (This system also has the advantage of keeping each of the brokers on their toes.)

At results time, the generally accepted and most workable format is to present the results to brokers' analysts first, then to hold a press briefing (in that order so that the Press can talk to the analysts when they get back to their offices) and then present them to the middle-level and junior fund managers.

The great benefit to brokers' analysts, fund managers and their analysts of meeting with the company's top team is the opportunity to mix with them informally after the presentation and seek out their own particular angles. This means, of course, that any disagreement or ignorance amongst the directors may be exposed, so there are risks. And remember that what everyone wants to know is: 'What's new?', 'What's different?' If nothing has changed, turn it into a virtue by explaining why, rather than leaving the impression of uninspired management.

Summary

It is worth repeating that, excluding special situations such as those covered in the next chapter, key elements of a good IR programme are planning and consistency. Decisions must be made about the amount of time and the number of people available for day-to-day IR and these resources must be used efficiently.

There is little point – indeed it will almost certainly be counter-productive – in including graphs in the annual report unless you are prepared to be equally communicative in a bad year.

Similarly, agreeing to attend a broker's lunch can cause massive offence to other brokers to whom you have refused similar access – unless you can justify the favouritism so objectively that any complainant runs the risk of you publicly exposing his lack of influence.

A series of lunches for fund managers this year could be a huge embarrassment to you next year if you decide not to continue with them. And the CEO may well cause enormous offence by agreeing to meet a small fund when the IR manager has restricted some of the middle-sized funds to seeing a lower-level director or manager.

Planning is the key; a regular, long-term programme which you commit the company to will earn the maximum respect. And open fairness about who meets whom and how often will avoid embarrassment, or even formal complaint.

CHAPTER 6

Prepare to repel borders
– *investor relations in special situations*

'**Prepare to repel borders – some Swiss company thinks it can take over!**'

'**Never fear, we'll get a brass band to play outside the House of Commons. That should rally the troops and send the gnomes back to their chalets.**'

The lesson of the last five years has been that companies must learn to communicate with their shareholders if they want to be safe from takeover. Of course, the sheer scale of difference between the pre-bid price and the ultimate winning bid makes it a tricky defence. But surely Rowntree, to take just one example, could have been defended if the company had set to work early enough and in the right way?

Instead of messing around with brass bands at Westminster when it was all over bar the shouting, Rowntree should have set to work much earlier at the slog of convincing people that they knew how to run it.

As Hamish McRae pointed out in *The Guardian* (June 1988), the company should have been able to convince shareholders that it was good at developing brands. Despite some scepticism for the current fad in financial markets for brand names, institutional investors looked to Rowntree to demonstrate its ability in brand management.

Instead, much of the defence actually took the form of condemning the City for not caring about the workers. Not only is that exceptionally stupid (if you want the City on your side you don't encourage tame MPs to be rude about it) but it is not credible. In any case, any shred of credibility that such a defence might have, was cut away by the workers' representative deciding in favour of the new ownership.

Hamish McRae also commented that Rowntree top management had been 'singularly unavailable' to the Press during the takeover. 'It is hard to think of any takeover battle in the last decade when the chairman has been so unavailable', he wrote. 'Viewed from a newspaper office, this failure to communicate is really very odd. It is almost as though they don't know what they are supposed to be doing,' he added.

Pre-empting the sentiment of this book, Mr McRae added that if companies do not bother to try and communicate, or if they choose leaders who are hopeless at the art of communication, they are in effect saying they feel no need to explain themselves to their owners. 'In this day and age, this is not only extraordinarily arrogant. It is also exceptionally unwise,' he concluded.

Effective communications are never more crucial than in crisis situations but, as in most cases, consistent communication, day in, day out, with investors and their advisers can prevent the crisis from arising in the first place. A record of consistent communication and credible deeds behind you can often save the day when, at first, all seems lost.

Financial crisis can take many forms. Apart from the unwanted takeover, it can involve recovering from a 'Black Monday' market crash; coping with a terrible industrial accident as Union Carbide had to after the Bhopal tragedy and Occidental Oil after Piper Alpha; reacting to a Budget containing unpleasant provisions in it which you failed to foresee, like the windfall profit tax on the banks; a long-running strike; the loss of a major order on which market hopes had been pinned, eg, British Aerospace's loss of the Tornedo order; the chairman suddenly dying; a credit ratings slide; a rights issue which no-one supports (Blue Arrow); a Monopolies and Mergers Commission report which tells you to sell most of your pubs – the list goes on. A look at Exxon's handling of the *Valdez* incident provides a salutary illustration of how *not* to do it. It's little wonder that some senior executives give it all up and become fishermen in the Orkneys!

Tracking issues

'An issue ignored is a crisis ensured,' Dr Henry Kissinger once said. Many potential financial crises can be prepared for by tracking what is being thought and planned by legislature in countries where you have operations. Having good government-monitoring systems in place can generally help you to keep pace with new laws being considered and present the company with opportunities to lobby against them, or make provision to accept them and sometimes turn them to competitive advantage. It will certainly help the IR manager to plan any review of his IR strategy that may need to be implemented. And tracking emerging investment methods and fashions can give similar advance warnings, as we have argued.

The moment of truth for companies finding themselves in 'special situations' is usually when they discover how successful (or otherwise) their IR effort has been; or when the fact comes sharply into focus that they have neglected one of the most important areas of corporate communication.

Dealing with takeovers

The chances of surviving a hostile bid have become steadily worse over the last six years of merger mania. But the characteristics of the company itself will usually provide clues as to its likely vulnerability to a takeover or its strength as a potential bidder. The most common vulnerability signs are:

- static or falling earnings
- poor return on capital
- unhealthy dividend policy
- bad cash management – or poor cashflow
- excessive gearing
- poor investment policy
- too many, difficult to justify, share issues
- unimaginative asset management (eg, over-stocked pension fund or cash mountain)
- major shareholder likely at any moment to sell off shares
- looming tax or protectionist legislation.

The predator signs are:

- business synergy with the predator (improved earnings prospects of the combined companies)
- cash mountain that has to go somewhere
- marketing synergy
- knocking out the victim as direct competition
- acquisition of management team
- acquiring extra production or distribution capacity.

The growing trend of leveraged bids by essentially financial bodies has added a further dimension and made it even more imperative for companies to be prepared. Badly run companies may no longer be the only targets if cashflow becomes the key criterion.

All listed companies should have contingency plans to fend off the unwanted takeover – and they should be rehearsed from time to time.

Regular discussions need to be held by the IR manager, merchant bank, brokers and public relations consultancy to review the probability of a bid and the company's ability to defend itself.

Much of the success or failure of the real thing (or rehearsal) will depend on how fast you can access your shareholders to explain your defence. The work done on the company's share tracking system will never prove more vital than now. Shareholder lists need names, addresses and telephone numbers.

The predator will nearly always have begun to build his or her stake in the company disguised through a whole series of nominee holdings. It is therefore essential that companies have built into their Articles of Association the right to disenfranchise nominee shareholders who won't disclose the investors' real identity under section 212 of the Companies Act. The law now even allows such holders to be banned from dividend payments and from selling the shares.

In a takeover situation it used to be the rule that the defending company could only talk to one institutional investor at the time on the grounds that giving collective briefings – because they could not include all the company's shareholders – meant that information was being unevenly distributed. In reality, however, this meant that companies were prone to being more indiscreet on a one-to-one basis, so the Takeover Panel changed the rules to allow collective briefings – so long as the company's merchant bank is present. One could, of course, argue that both systems are equally unfair to small funds and individuals – further supporting the view that the City is run *by* the City *for* the City. However, the current system certainly underlines the need for maintaining updated lists of the company's top 100 investors. A dedicated takeover or defence team should swing into action the moment a bid seems likely; and for the defence team this will often be last thing on a Friday evening or on a weekday dawn.

The teams will usually consist of the executive chairman or chief executive, FD, perhaps a third main board director, and the IR manager, with the company secretary closely involved. Outside advisors will include the company's merchant bank, broker, public relations consultant and legal advisor. In addition, one or more of the company's non-executive directors may have useful experience and objectivity.

Members need to be relieved from all their normal day-to-day activities during the takeover to allow them to concentrate solely on implementing the bid or defence strategy. Other directors – with one of them clearly in charge – and executives must be seen to be getting on with running the normal operations of the company. But the two teams should meet regularly to update each other.

It is *absolutely* essential that the IR manager constitutes part of the team and is not simply informed of decisions afterwards. He will have a key role to play in the successful conduct of the takeover since it is the manager who will be talking mostly to the financial media and brokers' analysts who, at this point, will be representing the main influences of opinion.

The IR manager (as opposed to the public relations manager if the two functions are distinct) will possess the background knowledge, be able to interpret relevant facts and figures, and play a crucial role in the successful outcome of the takeover – on whichever side he is sitting. But the company cannot afford to let the manager become out of date on investors' concerns or top management views.

Whether or not the takeover or defence is successful, the threat or opportunity of takeover will certainly energize the management on either side, which can produce great improvements in efficiency but, equally, can lead to the worst decisions of all. Cutting capital investment and other long-term projects in order to produce a short-term increase in profits may push up the share price and may make a company better armed or better insulated to achieve its ends – but at what cost over the long term? On the other hand, a takeover bid will often be a useful excuse for killing off a 'doubtful' long-term project which has always been somebody's favourite plaything.

The Takeover Panel will be watching every move made by the companies on either side. Part of the role of the IR manager, therefore, is to take the offensive at internal meetings and question each tactic being considered during the battle. Will the moves under consideration be adjudged to be in the best interests of shareholders? Could there be a DTI enquiry after the battle is over, even if it has been successful? Will the company's actions be defensible as well as credible when being explained to analysts and the media?

To a large extent, the IR manager's neck will be on the public and private chopping block if he fails to provide management with the best advice from an outsider's perspective. Part of his role, as we have already discussed, is to act as the company's antennae amongst the investment community as well as one of the company's principal mouthpieces to it.

The IR manager needs to be present at all investor meetings, whether large or small, because he can't take the risk of the CEO or CFO making statements which aren't being made to other investors. As well as that of protagonist, the IR manager must also be the co-ordinator of messages ensuring that no-one speaks with forked tongue, however inadvertently.

Timetable of a UK takeover

Companies that find themselves involved in takeovers will live by the following timetable, laid down by the Takeover Panel.

Day 0
The bidder publishes its offer document. This must come within 28 days of a firm intention to bid being announced.

Day 1
Shareholders of the target company can accept the offer from now on.

Day 14
The defence document must be posted.

Day 21
The bidder must say what acceptances have been received. If a majority of shareholders have not been won over, the company can withdraw, increase the offer, or extend the bid by periods of between seven and 14 days. Most bidders extend to a day after number 39 so they can have the last word.

Day 39
Deadline for publication of crucial evidence by the target company, including profit forecasts, proposed dividends and general performance.

Day 42
Shareholders who have accepted the first offer made by the bidder are free to change their minds.

Day 46
Last date for raising the bid. The bidder has one more week to attack its opponent, which is unable to respond. The offer remains open for another two weeks, during which time the bidder cannot raise its stake in the target company to more than 30 per cent.

Day 60
Decision day. All acceptances must be received by 3 pm, and the announcement of success or failure has to be made by 5 pm.

Two developments can disturb this timetable. First, another bidder may intervene. This usually leads to the Takeover Panel extending the deadlines to allow for disruption and extra work. Second, there can be a referral of the bid to the Monopolies and Mergers Commission. The Secretary of State for Trade and Industry can refer a merger at any time during the bid and in the six months after it has taken place. Under current government policies, a merger may be investigated by the Monopolies and Mergers Commission if the two companies together supply or consume over 25 per cent of goods or services in a UK sector, or the gross value of the worldwide assets taken over exceeds £30 million, or on 'national interest' grounds. On referral the bid falls, although a new bid may be permitted following the MMC investigation.

Some institutions are highly sensitive about talking to company managements in a takeover situation. The Norwich Union, for example, forbids it, preferring not to be subjected to contrary arguments directly while it is trying to make a sensitive decision. Others seem to delight in it!

Measures such as looking for a 'white knight' to ride in as your preferred, alternative bidder; court litigation; or encouraging a monopoly investigation at home or at EEC level may be the only means of salvation. But, again, these contingencies are better planned beforehand (see Boy scout drills, page 93).

Dirty tricks

For many years in America, firms of private detectives have been employed to go into every detail of the private and public lives of rival companies. There are specialist firms in New York which do little else. Nonetheless, the UK financial community is disturbed to find the dirty tricks brigade beginning to manifest itself in Britain too.

Hoylake, the vehicle through which a consortium headed by Sir James Goldsmith bid for BAT Industries in 1989, said that it 'deplored' the use of BAT shareholders' funds in the retention of 'detective agents at an undisclosed fee'. BAT responded by pointing out that the activities of the firm in question, Kroll Associates, would be restricted to financial investigation, particularly amongst companies with stakes in Hoylake who were based in countries 'where the disclosure requirements are not the same as in the UK'. The arguments ran that it was in the shareholders' interests to have the fullest possible information about the bidder.

During the bid by Argyll Group for Distillers in 1986, it was widely reported in the Press that a former employee of a company controlled by James Gulliver was approached by a man purporting to carry out 'international investigations'. The man wanted information about Gulliver and was reported to be willing to pay up to $10,000 if it was good enough to lose Gulliver his £2.5 billion bid for the whisky group.

The ex-Gulliver employee was aware of the significance of the approach. He recorded the conversation and sent the tape and a signed affidavit to one of Gulliver's right-hand men. James Gulliver was subsequently reported in the Press as saying: 'He has information which could only have come from Distillers or their advisors. It is the dirty tricks department at work. I have been followed for days, we have been under surveillance, and we know that people have been going over every detail of my personal life going back more than thirty years.'

Distillers denied that it had ever 'been concerned with the personal or private life' of Gulliver but, later, results of the investigations surfaced. After a press conference held by Distillers to discuss its latest takeover proposals, a copy of a document was 'selectively leaked' to several newspapers by persons as yet unknown. It showed that James Gulliver's entry in *Who's Who* was not strictly correct as he had never been a student at Harvard University – which is what the *Who's Who* entry implied.

Most City fund managers dismissed the news of Gulliver's academic record as irrelevant to the more serious issue of who had the best team to run Britain's biggest whisky company. But, according to a report in the *Sunday Times* shortly afterwards, one large investment company held a board meeting at the weekend and, according to one person there, spent some time discussing it: 'One director argued that it had nothing to do with the bid and should be ignored. But the man who actually invests the funds took a different line. He reckoned if Gulliver could be misleading about a little matter, he could be misleading about a bigger one.'

The increasing trend towards court litigation is regrettable because the Takeover Panel does provide a good framework in which to ensure 'fair play' on both sides without resorting to legal action – indeed the EEC is currently jumping through hoops to come up with a directive which retains the *status quo* and allows the Panel to continue its work without legal powers. (See table on page 158.)

And, when on the defence, you can always try to persuade the OFT to refer the bid to the Monopolies and Mergers Commission. (Not that a recommendation from the Commission is a final judgment by any means – the Minister can over-rule and the Commission can decide either way. But, in practice, a green light from the OFT will normally enable a takeover to go through, while a red one may well stop it – and certainly gives the victim a few months to prepare its defences.)

The OFT – whose boss, Sir Gordon Borrie, has been described as 'the person with the greatest influence over British industrial structure' – also has a formal role in negotiating under what circumstances a company *might* mount a bid for another, the idea being for the OFT to enable a company to frame a bid in such a way as to minimize any damage to competition.

So if a company wants a favourable wind from the authorities before making a bid, it can bargain with the OFT, perhaps about the bits that will be disposed of if it wins, before it has to commit itself.

In preparing for either a bid or defence, it is a more than sensible idea to ask an analyst from your corporate broker to look at all the arguments being prepared – particularly written material – and to tear through the worst excesses. This precautionary, and often revealing, measure will protect the company against the worst excesses of the merchant bankers who have helped in compiling the offer or defence documents.

Above all, it is vital to remember that the purpose of that document-ation during a takeover, whether aimed at investors, their advisors or the media, is to *communicate* the benefits, or otherwise, of the bid going through. They are *not* documents for lawyers, accountants and bankers to practice their gobbledegook English in.

Keep the latest information on the takeover available at all times to investors by using one of the independent telephone shareholder ser-vices. Licensed by the Stock Exchange, the organizations providing this service enable shareholders and other interested parties to call the company's own allocated number and hear the latest news supplied by the subscribing company in the early hours of each morning.

Ensure that, whenever relevant, other influential groups are encour-aged to speak out on your behalf. Employees, trade unions and MPs can help to influence the outcome depending on the extent to which they know and understand the company before the takeover. But, again, you are unlikely to win strong defenders if you never bothered to communicate with these groups until the bid came; the brass band outside the House of Commons will do little but arouse sceptism amongst MPs and entertain the tourists.

Boy scout drills

Above all, have your immediate actions planned in advance. It may be impossible to write a precise script for every possible variation of that first fateful telephone call. But some prior discussion should ensure that the first reaction does not lose the whole battle; here again, the CEO who answers his own telephone is a distinct liability. Nominating one spokesperson and having an absolute ban on anyone else discussing the bid (even with friends – clever bidders often seek personal routes to members of the board of their target) should ensure that messages are properly controlled, and still allows for the CEO to make a (properly prepared) call back. If it is not certain that the IR manager could handle this role, *now* is the time to replace him, not once the company is under fire.

Grounds for monopoly reference can be prepared, dossiers on likely bidders created, possible white knights discussed, hidden assets or arguments evaluated, legal defences briefed. Takeover rules prevent the initiation of major asset sales or purchases once a bid is made, unless shareholder assent is won. So preparation might involve identifying likely moves and recording a board minute that such action was under consideration. This would permit the company to go ahead under bid conditions (although one might ask why, if a division would be sold under bid conditions, it should not be sold now).

Market crash: company write-off?

Virtually all market antennae, let alone those of the IR function, were blind to, and temporarily blinded by, the black of that fateful Monday in October 1987. Although many talked of its possibility, like some impending South Sea Bubble, few, with the notable exception of Sir James Goldsmith, rubbed their eyes quickly enough to take precautionary action swiftly enough.

'Black Monday' was a ghastly experience for all affected by it – companies, investors and investment advisors alike. It was a lesson, like those served on companies who suffer terrible industrial accidents, of the need for better safety procedures. 'Black Monday' taught the investment world, rather expensively, of the need to read *long-term*, as well as prevailing, market conditions. The warnings were there in the small print for all to read but everyone was concentrating on the chapter headings.

Trends and fashions in the marketplace change all the time. In a bull market, everyone screams for earnings per share growth. In a bear market they want recurring revenue and solid dividend growth. For the IR manager, reading the signs is essential if he is going to be able not to change fundamentally, but alter the emphasis of, the IR message. Obviously, a company can't be shouting about its earnings per share (EPS) one minute, and its dividend performance the next. It needs a core message, a message which distinguishes itself from others to which it is compared, around which different emphasis can be placed.

It happens all the time in consumer marketing. If you were a chocolate manufacturer you might one day be extolling the product's taste differential; on another, depending on the fashion in the market, you might extoll the fact that it is artificial additives-free; but *all* the time you would be extolling the quality of the chocolate itself.

Investment fashions in the City change as fashions do in any other market. In 1986, megabids were all the rage, so companies went for megabids; but those mounting their bids towards the end of the trend either flopped (like BTR's bid for Pilkington) or just scraped through.

Megabids were replaced by management buyouts – although Sun Alliance's resistance to the Magnet buyout in 1989 indicates some doubts over this trend. The current trend, which may or may not take root, is for 'unbundling' – the highly leveraged bid for diversified companies where the cashflow or the asset values of the parts make them worth more than the whole.

Reading the market signs correctly should strongly influence the financial activities of companies, and enable them to capitalize on the trend as it climbs towards its peak. Excessive damage will be prevented for the company with sufficient vision to jump off at the top of the downward spiral and which has a core strategy strong enough to push it through the changes in fashion.

Industrial crisis

A major industrial crisis which causes loss of life or injury, or a long-running media story because of a pollution incident or strike will certainly weaken the company and may make it vulnerable to takeover.

But such crises are withstandable, as has been proved by, for instance, Union Carbide, Occidental Oil, and Johnson and Johnson. [Preparing for, and dealing with, such crises is a subject in itself: see *Crisis Management*, Michael Regester, Business Books, 1989.]

The investment community, and other interested parties, judge managements' ability to deal with the aftermath of such situations largely by what they see, hear and read in the media – so the media must become a focal point for information dissemination during a crisis of this nature. Indeed, the company that handles such a crisis well frequently *increases* investor loyalty rather than loses it.

Specifically, however, investors will want fast information about, for example, lost production capacity, insurance claims, and the length of time likely before things return to normal. They will want realistic assessments of likely loss of revenues over both the short and long term and knowledge of plans, if any, to cover the shortfall.

The IR manager will need a direct line of communication with the public relations people dealing with both operational management and the news media (he may not be able to reach operational management if it is a major disaster) to form fast responses to questions from investors; at all times the IR manager should be prepared to supplement facts about what has happened with the steps being taken by the company to deal with the situation and the likely long-term effects.

Here, too, preparation is the ideal. Preparing contingency plans for the more likely crises (much as we all like to think they won't happen) substantially increases the company's chances of coming through the crisis well. IR is, in these cases, a secondary, but still important, part of the preparation.

Credit ratings slide

As debt becomes an increasingly important way for companies to raise finance – especially during a bear market – a drop in the rating given to the company by one of the credit ratings agencies can severely restrict the company's ability to raise additional debt on the most competitive terms and so penalize long-term growth prospects. The significance of credit ratings, and how they are obtained, remains one of the greatest areas of ignorance among IR managers, and often among their CEOs and many analysts too; so we will explain their value before discussing how to deal with a drop in the rating you have been given.

Credit ratings – generally sought from the two main credit ratings agencies, Standard & Poors and Moodys – come down to confidence in the company's ability to service its debt.

Officials from the credit rating agencies are less interested in earnings per share growth or any of the other indicators so favoured by the equity analyst. They simply look for three to five year's worth of projected borrowings (ie, cost of borrowing) and projected profit over the same period, to cover the interest rates, as well as the degree of asset-backing or stand-by credit.

The dilemma lies in giving management's long-term forecasts to a particular group of people when, if you embarked on such an exercise with anyone else, it would be judged as providing insider information of the most sensitive kind. For this reason, and understandably, company lawyers and accountants become very agitated when examining information which it is proposed should be put forward to these agencies. But credit ratings agencies wouldn't exist if they didn't guarantee absolute confidentiality, so lawyers and accountants have no real need to get into a frenzy – at least, if you discount the moral argument. So, on the face of it, credit ratings provide a totally objective measure of the company's likely future performance, based on information that will never be released to the more usual audiences for IR activity. That said, the agencies' reliability has been called into question by a few notable failures.

As the credit and equity markets become increasingly blurred (ie, 'the securitization of debt') so credit ratings, based on detailed and confidential information, can easily provide useful reassurance to investors (although analysts will normally only appreciate this if it is pointed out to them). Since the credit rating agency is looking at interest cover, cashflow and credit-backing, its assessment certainly does not cover all of the factors an equity analyst is interested in; nevertheless, it is taking a detailed view and passing a judgment from a position of experience and superior information. In any case, in the era of the leveraged bid, a credit-rating is close to an assessment of ultimate value, since the leveraged bid works mainly through cashflow and interest cover.

Maintaining or improving the company's credit rating does not depend on making just an annual presentation but on keeping the credit rating agencies consistently informed of the company's progress and performance. They have to be able to give a 365-day assessment of the company's credit worthiness. Should they ever learn that the company has become unreliable – for example, by avoiding them if the company's affairs start to go wrong – then it will take years to win back their confidence and you may see your rating slide along with all the hard work that was put into winning the rating in the first place.

So the first step is to prevent the rating slipping in the first place. If the agencies are briefed in advance of every significant move the company is about to make (erring on the side of caution) they may well have the confidence not to downgrade the rating even when there's been a blip in the company's cashflow situation.

Today, debt financing is an ever-more important part of overall funding, since it depends on much more than keeping one bank manager sweet. An IR manager cannot afford to ignore debt as a direct substitute for equity and he should be involved in all relationships with the analyst-equivalent, the credit-rating agencies. Only then can the manager not only ensure that those all-important relationships prosper, but also be much better able to handle the effect on the equity markets if disaster falls and the rating is downgraded. At the very least, he will know about the likely downgrading far enough in advance to be able to prepare plans.

Convertible debt – IR or treasury responsibility?

The securitization of debt can create other tensions. If the company decides to issue a form of debt convertible into equity – such as convertible Eurobonds – there will need to be careful co-operation between the treasury and IR teams. After all, bonds are generally sold through banks to corporate treasurers, other banks, etc. As such, the treasurer may argue that they are sold on price and terms, with little need for company image to be boosted in these audiences. But this is an unbalanced argument, since the rates achieved in these markets can be clearly shown to be affected by company image.

However, the debt will probably convert to equity at some stage, and it will, therefore, 'overhang' the equity market in the meantime. Analysts will include it in calculating 'fully diluted' earnings per share; Investor Protection Committees (IPCs) will include the shares in their calculation of your issue limits, so it will affect the amount of equity available to you immediately, even though it will not become equity for some time; and any bonds not sold to owners who intend to retain the equity will flow back into the equity markets, depressing the share price.

The IR manager, then, not only needs to explain to shareholders why this is the best form of funding; he must also ensure that the bonds go to potential shareholders, and needs to plan a campaign persuading them to retain the shares. He will need to treat the original issue as if it were equity and the owners as important potential shareholders, so close co-operation with the treasury team will be essential.

The same applies, to some extent, to other forms of debt or preference shares. The IR manager cannot afford to ignore them, even if they are sold to different markets and are not convertible. They are an alternative to equity and the manager needs to be able to explain why the company chose the instrument and how it affects the board's future equity plans.

Equity issues – whose rights count?

Companies deciding to raise new capital by issuing more ordinary shares face a range of difficult decisions and restrictions. In the UK, they are restricted by law to issuing such shares only to existing shareholders (who have so-called 'pre-emption rights') unless they have obtained shareholder consent at an AGM or EGM to withdraw these rights. But here, the IPCs of the major institutional shareholder associations – primarily the National Association of Pension Funds and the Association of British Insurers – impose further limits. These have no legal standing but they threaten opposition by their members to any issue breaching their guidelines.

Summary of IPC guidelines

- Companies can ask shareholders for an annual withdrawal of five per cent of issued capital, but should not use more than 7.5 per cent in any rolling three-year period without consulting the IPC.
- The rate of discount at which equity is issued for cash other than to existing shareholders should not exceed five per cent, including commissions as well as any market discount.

(Detailed clarification of the guidelines can be obtained from the Stock Exchange.)

If it decides to stick to the existing shareholder route – the 'rights issue' – a company has two choices: either to have the issue underwritten by a firm of brokers who guarantees to take up any shares which are not subscribed for; or to do a 'deeply discounted' rights issue which is not underwritten by a third party.

While going the 'underwritten' route is obviously 'safer' for the company, it suffers from the drawback of underwriters' fees, and the fact that any unsubscribed shares will be acquired by the underwriters' broker at a discounted price – further concentrating share ownership.

On the face of it, therefore, it might seem in the shareholders' best interests not to have the new issue underwritten, so saving the company possibly millions of pounds in fees. But going the 'deeply discounted' route may mean that the shares do not all sell, or that they sell at a price which negates the management's plans for the proceeds – and which drags the price of the existing shares down too.

The nub of the problem is the division between what the company wants to achieve versus what the shareholders want – and under company law, companies still need to act in 'the best interests of the company', ie shareholders *and* employees.

For some curious reason, a company can issue shares to pay for an acquisition without the existing shareholders having any pre-emption rights. Hence, one reason for growth by acquisition – in these cases, management can sell new shares to anyone they like (the so-called 'vendor placing').

But if it wishes to raise cash, the board is assumed to be less capable of acting responsibly and must comply with the restriction outlined above. Any issue of shares at net prices significantly below the current market price will dilute earnings per share – and hence the company's rating and future funding ability. So the discount must be included as cost of capital, along with the fees, and may well increase the returns required from the planned investment beyond those expected. Even if this is not the case, the concentration of ownership issue may well be a concern.

For these reasons, companies have been keen to avoid rights issues by using other financial instruments (debt, convertibles, preference shares, etc) or by expanding through acquisition. But the IPC guidelines do allow companies to exceed their limits if sufficient justification is given (see also Chapter 7 on foreign issues).

Whatever form of funding is used, the IR manager needs to be able to explain the decision. If he cannot persuade shareholders that the investment is right for the company, and that the form of funding is right for the investment, then he is wrong for the job, or the plan is wrong for the company. Shareholders need to know what the investment and the form of funding implies for their shares. This explanation is not the job of lawyers and accountants; the IR manager needs to anticipate the concerns and prepare literature and presentations to cover them.

IR and the competition issue

As 1 January 1993 draws nearer, many companies are looking around for suitable European partners to strengthen their European trading positions and to insulate them from becoming another Rowntree – the subject of a successful takeover by a European predator.

There are some sectors where the rationalization of European industry is essentially complete. The motor industry is one: it is a virtually integrated industry in that you cannot tell in which country the car you are buying is made. But if some industries are already integrated across Europe, while others, like publishing and broadcasting, are starting to form cross-European alliances, there are industries where integration has hardly begun – which gives yet another dimension to the IR manager's role as the company's investor antennae. How vulnerable is your company's sector to European integration moves?

Retail financial services is one striking example. We drive around in cars made in France or Germany, buy magazines owned by Dutch companies, but we keep our bank account in a tru-Brit enterprise like NatWest or the Halifax – but for how much longer?

On the other hand, powerful arguments have been made for British insurance companies to expand into Europe. Southern Europe, in particular, is short on life assurance and the UK has enormous experience in this sector. So the logic would be to buy a Spanish insurance group and develop it into something really big . . . and so on.

EC rules which will govern mergers and acquisitions have yet to be formalized but, clearly, part of IR from now on will be maintaining an advanced view.

At the time of writing, the European Commission is proposing to look at any mergers of companies involving over 2bn Ecus in *combined* worldwide turnover. It will ignore mergers of companies, however, if two thirds or more of the turnover of the companies involved is in one country. Acquisitions of companies involving less than 100m Ecus are also unlikely to be the subject of scrutiny.

Once whatever EC mergers and acquisitions regulations are in place, the job of message co-ordination for the IR manager will become that much greater. The same arguments put forward to EC regulatory bodies will have to be put to Britain's Monopolies and Mergers Commission – not least for the reason that the MMC publishes its reports and EC officialdom will scrutinize them for any inconsistencies.

In addition, the single European market is bound to put extra political pressure on the already politically-sensitive OFT and DTI, so any steps a company can take to encourage the media, analysts and others to justify any reduction in competition (in other words to convince the OFT that it is not being led into more political flak) is bound to gain a big advantage.

The chairman is dead – long live the chairman

Somewhat morbidly, the first issue of the Economist's *Investor Relations* magazine led with an article explaining the IR role should the chairman suddenly die. While full of good advice, the issue really boils down to the fact that the chairman's death will only cause a problem with investors if he has been too closely identified with the company's success.

If the IR programme has successfully put across the company's management strength, the death or resignation of the chairman – or any other director – should have little long-term impact. This failure was presumably another reason for BTR's recent search for an IR manager – the company was seen, rightly or wrongly, to be totally dependent on Owen Green.

Here too, though, sensible contingency planning is worthwhile. You may have to accept that if half the board is killed in an air crash (most companies – or their insurers – will forbid the whole board from travelling together), little can be done except to weather the storm and play up the competence of the next management level. But some thought should be given to preparing for the loss of the chairman, CEO or any other key personality.

Summary

The message throughout, then, is that while much of the IR role consists of reacting to questions and events, the successful IR manager will have prepared himself – and his colleagues – for all foreseeable possibilities. He will have used all of the company's resources – internal experts and external advisers – to keep informed of all planned or potential issues; and will have initiated, if not carried out, preparation for all of the crises covered here, and any others he can think of. He will have involved several different kinds of management in the IR programme so that their support at a time of crisis will be credible and rehearsed; and will be ready to argue where necessary to ensure that clear, concise explanations can be given to shareholders for every decision.

Plenty of chairmen and CEOs die a business death long before a natural one because of their identification with a company's success which latterly turns sour – Tony Berry at Blue Arrow, George Davies at Next, Sir Clive Sinclair of C5 fiasco fame, to name only a few. Like the woman scorned, the investor who has suffered from the disappointment of management-inspired expectations can be expected to show his fury.

PART III

WIDER HORIZONS – INTERNATIONAL INVESTOR RELATIONS

CHAPTER 7

But they're all foreigners!
– costs and benefits of international IR programmes

Turning to his only colleague in a room full of 23 US lawyers, accountants and investment bankers, now going into their third day of 'due diligence' ahead of the company's US share issue, the finance director says: 'Can we capitalize the fees for all these people as part of the costs of issue?' The answer, of course, is yes; but would the existing shareholders – assuming they knew about it – approve of this use of *their* money to dilute their holding?

About 1,000 companies have listed their shares outside their home countries – representing approximately 2,000 listings on the world's top 22 exchanges – despite the differences in reporting and accounting regulations, tax and stamp duty difficulties, costs and effort involved. Why have they, and is the trend continuing or slowing?

The war of words wages on about the value of international listings – particularly in the UK, where, as we've seen, pre-emption rights give regulatory backing to the concentration of shareholdings in a diminishing number of hands – controlled by an ever smaller number of fund management groups.

On the one hand, shareholders can – and sometimes do – argue that their money is being spent on diluting their holdings and that they have supported the company since its public debut, so there is no reason to think that they will not continue to do so. This is why the Investor Protection Committees (IPCs) of the main institutional associations have imposed strict guidelines limiting the extent to which companies will be allowed to avoid pre-emption rights (see Chapter 1) and they are particularly resentful of the legal, accountancy and other costs of overseas issues – especially the fees to investment banks.

On the other hand, some companies can argue that there are numerous business reasons for overseas listings and issues, that concentration of shareholdings – and, even more so, of influence, given the trend towards specialist fund management – has gone far enough and that, in any case, if an issue of shares is involved, the new shareholders are paying the costs of the issue. Moreover, a 20 per cent plus discount, which may be necessary in a rights issue, could easily destroy the viability of an acquisition, and overseas issues – with all their costs – are generally much cheaper for the company.

There is, of course, some justification for all of these views. Trading in Barclays Bank shares in Tokyo certainly does not justify the costs of the listing, but increased visibility and credibility in the world's largest financial market probably does. The same kind of reasoning no doubt applies to Nomura's recent listing in London. The Blue Arrow flop says little for the efficiency of the rights issue and even less for the credibility of the securities houses involved – both part of large fund management houses.

But there is no doubt that the IPCs are right to criticize some companies who have rushed into expensive issues and listings with no apparent objective other than to be dedicated followers of fashion. Others have declared sensible objectives but have not adequately assessed or addressed the investor relations needs of the new market and have therefore failed to make any long-term impact, so that the money spent has clearly been wasted.

The IPC guidelines do, in fact, have let-out clauses which permit breaches of their pre-emption limits if the case is properly argued – which places the onus where it ought to be: on the management's IR effort.

The argument is less to do with whether the guidelines are fair in detail, and more to do with the need for them in the first place and the impression given that the company is on the defensive from the first step. It can sometimes seem that the IPC argument is akin to that of a man who buys a newly-built house and then objects to a planning application by his neighbour opposite to split his site and build a second house on it. Surely in an efficient market, the disgruntled owner can always sell. And is it fair to limit the management's right to issue new shares for cash, but not their ability to issue greater amounts in an acquisition?

Statistics certainly show that overseas listings rarely generate huge trading volumes – at least, not in the short term. So how are the financial and operational costs of an international IR programme justified?

Reasons for overseas IR programmes

There is no doubt that some overseas listings have been initiated for the wrong reason, such as the chairman's ego, the CEO's ego, the appetite of the chairman's wife for Paris fashions, the fact that the CEO's son now lives in New York, and so on. But there are a number of less frivolous objectives which may apply in any particular case and these bear examination before we go on to look at the investor relations requirements involved:

- Increased funding options through global and regional (eg, EEC) security markets.
- Increased valuations in home and overseas markets.
- Support for acquisition programmes.
- Support for existing business operations.
- Encouragement of employee share ownership.

The first two of these are probably the most contentious and have a lot to do with that old chestnut 'the global securities market'.

The global securities market – fact or fiction?

The growing sophistication of communications media and investment analysis, and with changing economic patterns – together with reduced regulation in the major markets – has concentrated more minds on international comparisons of investment performance. Equity and debt investments are replacing physical assets like gold in international capital flows just as money replaced barter. But does a global securities market exist or not?

Well, it certainly does in the debt market – and too many of us tend to think of investor relations being purely about equity. In the days – dare one say the good old days? – when company borrowings were arranged over lunch at the bank, that was reasonable. But now, most of us probably raise money through bonds, commercial paper and the like. And they're bought by corporate treasurers and investment institutions. Increasingly, you'll need to be rated by a US credit rating agency if you want the best rates – and once you are, your debt will be traded worldwide (see credit ratings in Chapter 6). The increasing use of convertible shares, leveraged buy-outs and so on is blurring the distinction between debt and equity too, so these global habits are bound to spread.

And the equity market *is* becoming more international, whatever the cynics say. Salomon Brothers estimate that cross-border equity holdings total about $640 billion – 6.4 per cent of the world market's capitalization. US pension funds may have less than five per cent of their money in overseas equities, but nearly a quarter of all the US funds with over a billion dollars under management had reached the ten per cent mark last year – *excluding* their ADR holdings.

In 1987, euro-equities doubled; eight per cent of new issues by US companies were outside the USA; and 19 cross-border mergers exceeded $1 billion. Cross-border investment flows peaked at $33 billion in the first nine months of 1987.

In the three months following Black Monday, $32 billion of overseas investment money was pulled back into its home countries, and we were told the global market was dead. But that only took out *that year's* international investment, leaving all of the previous outflows in place. And in 1988, most of it flowed back into foreign markets. 1989 is widely expected to break all previous records with net cross-border flows totalling $40–50 billion.

Performance measurements for fund management firms are becoming increasingly international, and many have been deeply embarrassed by missing out on growth in the fastest moving markets – leaving their performance lagging behind the Goldman Sachs and other global indices.

Furthermore, leveraged buy-outs and company share repurchases – particularly in the USA and UK – are taking massive chunks of equity out of the market altogether – $125 billion worth in 1988 in the US alone – leaving more money chasing fewer shares around the world.

The 30 top investment bodies have already agreed to a number of measures to begin to harmonize securities regulation, and we should not fool ourselves that they will not keep the process going.

Even if the global market is slow to really take off, we are certainly going to see regional markets such as the EEC becoming more important. The EEC represents a quarter of the entire world equity market and harmonization has already started. We have already seen the introduction of EEC listing requirements; other measures are well underway, with the abolition of exchange controls already agreed for 1992 – with eight countries jumping the gun by July 1990 – and a new stock market proposed to unify trading in large European companies.

When Margaret Thatcher's government lifted exchange controls in the UK in its first year in power, 20 per cent of UK investment funds flowed overseas almost overnight, a vivid demonstration not only of the international horizons of UK investment managers but also of the pressure of international competition. The UK finance directors who realized the implications of this (not many, apparently) could be forgiven for deciding that, if a fifth of the funds which would previously have been invested in the UK were now going abroad, they would seek alternative funds overseas in the future.

UK investors still account for roughly 20 per cent of all cross-border investment and, indeed, Europe as a whole has largely supplied most of its own capital needs in the last year or two. The Americans and Japanese have mainly invested in each other's companies, but both now have their eyes on Europe to take advantage of the re-structuring up to 1992 and beyond. So it's not difficult to imagine what might happen when all other barriers come down: many European institutions have suffered restrictions on foreign investment, and their pensioners, policy-holders, etc, have had to put up with their consequent under-performance. The pressure on the fund managers will surely be intense, and we have already seen the beginning of what could become a huge consolidation, creating pan-European fund management groups for us all to learn to live with.

The IR implications of this multi-language market are a nightmare and probably explain the (sometimes frenzied) attempts being made to form a European IR federation, involving bodies such as the UK's Investor Relations Society which is helping its members to cope with this emerging environment. (After all, the IRS still has by far the world's highest proportion of members with international experience.)

It surely cannot be long before someone creates a really valid European equivalent to the FT indices and to the Stock Exchange's alpha-stock classification, whether it is based on co-operation between the existing exchanges or on an outside initiative (by Reuters or the like). Despite the complexities and different accounting conventions and investment criteria, we must see the emergence of regional and global indices and top-stock classes, which will permit passive (index-linked) investment by institutions who give up the expensive struggle to out-perform in such a complex and competitive market. Indeed several global indices are already fighting for recognition.

So companies will have to make the choice between promoting themselves as global stocks or being relegated to national niche markets; the bigger ones will not even have the choice. But we will all have to recognize that we are competing for capital in a global – or, at least, regional – market. Some will become the equity market equivalents to Distillers and some to Guinness. The difference is what international IR is largely about.

Whether it is global indices or credit ratings that make the money managers feel safe about venturing into overseas instruments, we can be sure it will happen and companies which have no policies and machinery for satisfying the information needs it generates will wish they had been better prepared.

Acquisitions – has the target ever heard of you?

The company which aims to expand by overseas acquisitions faces various problems. Unless its name is already known through its products, the chairman's request for a meeting with the target company will probably be greeted with a 'Who the . . . is he?' Worse, if an offer goes ahead, it may well be met with a resounding yawn by the target shareholders and rank hostility from its employees. Lord Hanson certainly cannot have enjoyed the public mauling he was subjected to by SCM, and both Blue Arrow and WPP suffered serious staff hostility. All three succeeded with their bids but surely they would have incurred lower personal and financial costs if they had not been so ruthless (and less unloved). By contrast, John Makinson may not have been greeted with open arms when he, as Saatchi's US acquisition man, went to visit potential targets, but he didn't have to spend his first half-hour explaining who Saatchi were or what were their objectives.

Nestlé, Bond Corporation and Minorco are other examples of companies which have recently faced hostility over foreign bids. But these, and the others mentioned above, were all offering cash. How much *more* difficult would they have found it if they had been offering shares, given that most of them had done little IR beforehand? LEP group became the first foreign company, in 1988, to make a US acquisition entirely for shares and BET did the first cross-border vendor placing in Europe early in 1989.

Increased valuation – unlikely in the short term

Until truly comparable financial standards are introduced, making a real global index possible, national markets will continue to operate on different criteria, with companies valued very differently.

Average price-earnings ratios (PERs) at time of writing stood at 66.1 in Tokyo, 13.5 in New York and 11.5 in London. This, of course, prompts the naive director to look at PERs for comparable companies on other markets and assume that a listing there would win his company a similarly high rating – making acquisitions cheaper, employee share schemes more successful, the company less vulnerable, etc.

There are two cautionary notes to be sounded here. First, accounting changes must be taken into account. As we shall see ('Can your accountants cope', page 114), these can substantially change the company's reported earnings in the foreign market, so that its existing share price represents a multiple much closer to its foreign peers already. BET shares, for example, traded at a PER of about 12 in June 1989 but its US earnings – after US accounting changes – were nearly

30 per cent below those in the UK, so its PER in New York was already 15 or 16, compared to 17 or 18 for its counterparts.

Second, it will take some time for a foreign share to develop a trading market abroad active enough to affect its domestic value. As in any market, prices depend largely on overall demand, so the valuation of the company *can* be changed if IR helps to increase demand for the shares – at home or abroad. But international investors are sophisticated enough to recognize really significant valuation differences, so an overseas listing will bring no immediate change.

We will almost certainly see more foreign acquisitions made through shares as international trading develops. Shortages of equity in the USA make foreign shares increasingly acceptable and, even if acquisition activity does not grow in Tokyo (and many think it will), the single market in Europe is widely expected to increase bid levels in the EEC. French commissioner Jacques Delors was recently quoted as predicting that 10,000 French companies will merge with foreign companies before 1992!

Contrast the Nestlé bid for Rowntree and the Bond bid for Lonhro with the Minorco bid for Consolidated Goldfields and the value of understanding the target and its environment, and of careful positioning and execution of communication, are clearer.

Certainly, if shares are to be used as consideration, they will be poorly received if they cannot be traded locally and come from a little-known company. And in many markets – such as the USA – it would be impossible to register the shares in time (see US markets, Chapter 8).

IR, then, can play an important role in preparing the ground for a bid – or, of course, for a defence. But it can also help in identifying targets in the first place. Bankers who have intimate knowledge of suitable targets will not be forming queues outside the head offices of unfamiliar companies. You may see them when they've hawked an unwanted business-for-sale around all their favourites in vain, and reached desperation point. But they're only going to bring you their choicest morsels if they know you and your strategy well enough to put you at the top of their list of likely buyers. And you'll only be their *first* call if their analyst also covers you, their traders make money on your shares, and they are confident they can raise the money for you – and make a fat fee in the process!

Your business operations – are they on their own?

Stories abound of salesmen in foreign parts climbing mountains just to reach level ground. Potential customers have been told by your competitor that you're a foreign, asset-stripping shark; they shouldn't give the deal to your subsidiary because you'll have run it into the ground before the contract is complete. Or said competitor suggests Mr Prospect looks your subsidiary up on the Dun & Bradstreet credit database to see if it's creditworthy.

The truth is, of course, that you're a long-term builder of businesses who is investing in improving the subsidiary – not running it down, and your absence from the D&B database is not because you're not reliable or stable enough but because they seldom cover unlisted foreign companies. But your salesman probably doesn't know these things, and has lost the contract before he starts.

Having your shares listed daily in the local newspapers, your details entered on key business and financial databases, and your company known by local bankers can be an immeasurable help to your overseas operations. It indicates that you take the market seriously and that you are there to stay. In some markets (like the USA) your key customers are probably investors too, so a favourable broker's report may give your subsidiaries a further boost. If you are listed on the local stock exchange, many customers probably won't even know you are a foreign company. Finally, the senior executives can always combine some useful customer relations with their IR roadshows.

Employees – will they benefit?

The virtues of employee share ownership are becoming increasingly well-known and many companies now have widespread executive and employee share option and ownership schemes. They are important to staff motivation and loyalty and are becoming a favourite means of bid-protection – particularly in the USA.

But shares and share options are of severely limited value to staff if they cannot monitor their performance, obtain advice from local stockbrokers and trade them in their local market. Executives may have the ability to overcome these problems – though many don't – but other employees almost certainly won't.

The twice annual dividend distribution and reports can be a useful way to by-pass local managers who are obstructing other forms of company communication. And if employee presentations are added to the IR roadshows, an even more useful link is created.

In people-based companies, IR can play an important part in employee morale and loyalty. BET listed its shares in New York in 1987 and launched what is believed to be the country's first ADR-based employee share ownership plan in 1988. A programme of directors' visits to more than 25 of the company's sites during an investor/customer/staff roadshow, plus a widely-distributed video, hugely improved morale and resulted in 37 per cent of all eligible employees joining the scheme in the first year alone. The company listed its shares on three continental European exchanges in 1988 and is working on a pan-European employee share plan for launch in 1989.

The gradualist approach

Increasing international investment in your company may not, of course, necessitate the rigours of international travel. For example, 65 per cent of US pension funds' investment in foreign equities is managed by offshore fund managers – principally in London. The big Japanese funds do virtually all their overseas trading through cheaper foreign exchanges. The UK-based company has a starting point of over 500 foreign banks with offices in London. Stock Exchange statistics show that about 15 per cent of all purchases of UK equity through London are made by foreign investors.

Many of the world's largest fund managers (eg, Fidelity and Nomura) have investment teams in the City and most of the international securities houses will drool over any company which lets it be known that it has a new policy of attracting foreign investment – they will soon submerge the IR manager with requests to bring in this visiting US fund or that Japanese investor.

The situation is similar – though perhaps slightly less simple – in most other major foreign cities in Europe, and this is probably the best starting point for the IR manager with time on his side but little foreign experience. A year of meetings with foreign fund managers, on his own turf, should give his firm a good base to start from and will certainly give his management team invaluable exposure to the different styles of foreigners. The contrast between the US analyst's focus on cashflow and interest cover and the Japanese concentration on dividend yield – or whatever are the current fashions for each of them – can often be startling and unsettling, but may hold real opportunities which might have been missed in the headlong rush into overseas roadshows.

Indeed, many of the 2,000 foreign listings companies currently have are probably expensive ego trips – and often embarrassingly public ones, because the trading volume and shareholder records are often available to all. If you are only looking for extra funding or wider ownership, it will almost certainly be easier and cheaper to do a foreign IR programme in your own country.

Taking the plunge

When this preparatory period is over – or earlier for the impatient, the foolhardy or those without the option – you may conclude that the time has come for the mountain to go to Mohammed. Again, the gradualist approach is wiser if you have time on your side – pick one limited overseas market and try your skills there rather than risking a global flop.

At this stage, a whole range of new considerations come into play, which can be briefly summarized as follows:

- international financial reporting differences
- advisers – banks, lawyers, accountants and consultants
- logistics – venues, equipment, etc.
- presentations – content and language
- flowback – measurement of failure or greed
- costs and benefits – is it all worth it?
- listings and issues – what is the verdict?
- which market?

Can your accountants cope?

The first problem with any foreign exposure – it may have already surfaced during discussions at home with foreign investors – is the issue of comparability of financial information.

So far, the International Accounting Standards Committee (IASC) has made limited progress in persuading number-crunchers to produce comparable figures. Even the frequency of reporting differs, with the US Securities and Exchange Commission (SEC) requiring quarterly results to be reported within 45 days (but not, now, for foreign companies – see Chapter 8) while several European countries are still satisfied with one annual report and allow up to six months for it to be filed. And, worse, the basis of accounting shows wide variation.

The Americans complain that the ability of British companies to write off goodwill against shareholder reserves immediately on acquisition has given them a massive advantage over US firms – who have to depreciate goodwill against profits for up to 40 years – especially in acquiring US-owned service companies (with their low asset bases and thus high goodwill).

Some British FDs retort that the other side of this coin is that UK companies are left with apparently weaker balance sheets than their US counterparts because their intangible assets have been written off instead of put on the balance sheet (hence the current UK debate about including brand values on the balance sheet).

Whether acquired companies should be worth up to 90 per cent less today than they were yesterday (under UK accounting policies) or should be depreciated when they may be expanding (under US policies) is an argument for theorists. For the rest of us, the problem is that these – and many other – differences in Generally Accepted Accounting Principles (GAAP) between countries probably go a long way towards explaining the slow progress in international equity investment.

Consistency in financial reporting

The International Accounting Standards Committee (IASC) has listed a number of 'preferred treatments' to make financial statements of companies in different countries more comparable. They include:

- Goodwill should be written off against profits over five years, though this can be stretched to 20 years in exceptional circumstances.

Currently, US companies are allowed a 40-year write-off period while their counterparts take goodwill through reserves without touching future profits.

To comply with the IASC rule, companies would have to restate their profits in their main accounts to reflect the faster depreciation. UK companies, on the other hand, would need only to produce a footnote showing what *would* have happened if they had used this treatment – although the UK Accounting Standards Committee has now proposed to bring UK standards fully in line with the IASC goodwill standard. Whether UK FDs will comply is another matter.

- When valuing inventories, companies should assume that the first stocks produced or bought are the first ones to be sold.

This valuation method, known as first in first out, or FIFO, and used in most countries, contrasts with the LIFO method used in the US, which can lead to a considerable understatement of profits and inventories shown in balance sheets. US companies will be able to continue their current practice, provided they disclose the effects of a FIFO valuation method.

- Assets should be shown at cost rather than present values. Companies using revaluations in their accounts should disclose the historic cost in a note.

In a separate move, the IASC has agreed a draft standard on accounting for deferred taxes. In effect this would force companies in some countries, such as the UK and Ireland, to set aside far larger provisions for deferred taxes than at present, eating into their reported shareholders' funds.

To achieve a true understanding of your performance abroad, then, your accountants will have to take your last five years' carefully constructed accounts apart and put them together in a totally different way. In extreme cases (see Chapters 8 and 9) this may add £billions to the UK balance sheet but reduce its earnings per share by 25 per cent or more. So those high ratings for comparable companies in the USA and Japan may be an illusion!

Different accounting treatments

When Volkswagen decided to list its shares in London (as well as in Japan and the USA) invitees to the roadshow were disappointed by a corporate review which seemed to add little to their existing knowledge. It was two weeks before analysts discovered – in the small print of the prospectuses – that VW had given a reconciliation to UK GAAP, which exposed performance data never previously published, including an 11 per cent increase in EPS for 1987 which lifted 1988 EPS estimates by up to 25 per cent.

At the time, Adrian Cowell, chairman of Ark Securities and a noted expert in comparing international accounting standards, commented: 'Continental companies, generally speaking, are paying too much for their equity. If you are hiding your light under a bushel for various good domestic tax reasons, you can't raise equity on the same terms that American or British companies can. It is absolutely essential to IR since the cost of capital is key to being competitive on the international scene – something that continental companies are slowly beginning to perceive.'

The case of Telefonica's New York Stock Exchange listing in 1986 offers quite a different perspective. While undergoing a similar reconciliation process to VW's, providing instead a US GAAP statement of earnings, it chose rather to highlight the deviations between national and international assessments.

For years Telefonica had been allowed by the Spanish Government to revalue its assets, declare a lower profit, and therefore pay less tax. The change came when Telefonica got a NYSE listing and, after redrawing accounts on an historic basis and showing what historic depreciation costs and profits would be after the much smaller depreciation charge (which was in fact double), it suddenly appeared to American investors as if it were a US company – putting it on all fours, as it were, with US companies of the same kind. When profits in US terms were seen as high, investors bought a lot of stock.

Hanson Trust's accountants are said to have taken two years to prepare US GAAP accounts and BET admits to at least 12 months' concentrated work. The need to adjust for all the different and extra requirements, not only for the company as a whole but separately for every subsidiary acquired in the previous five years, is a huge task – and the need to have the new figures audited adds time (and cost) penalties.

Yet the new figures can markedly improve understanding, not only in the international marketplace, but also at home. Arguably, the exposure of the finance team to the first set of international accounting differences can increase their experience and their ability to meet other countries' requirements. Certainly, companies who have already undertaken this challenge will be better able to cope with future changes in reporting standards.

What value good advice?

The second great challenge on the road to global recognition and funding flexibility will be to assemble a suitable team of advisers. The lucky (or clever) company will have existing relationships with international banks, lawyers and consultants who would eagerly undertake to 'fix everything'.

Accepting such an offer may be a mistake. First, the reduced need for the IR team to research its chosen market itself could make it much less able to judge the advice it is getting – after all, if only a tiny minority of companies has so far initiated international IR, then *none* of the banks has that much experience and most of their staff have none. And anyway, every case is different.

Second, there is nothing like a 'beauty parade' to make the adviser wheel out its very best team and make extravagant promises of top performance – which you *may* be able to hold it to.

Third, listening to competing advisers – or, even better sometimes, appointing two competitors to work together – can give the IR team a valuable collection of best practices and keep all the advisers on their toes.

It would be folly to contemplate a major IR programme in the USA without consulting Goldman Sachs, Merrill Lynch, Shearson Lehman, Morgan Stanley, First Boston, etc. But no single band (and certainly no individual) has a monopoly on knowledge. Handling your long-term build-up bears no resemblance to advising HMG on the big-budget British Telecom give-away, but you will probably hear plenty of their war stories – some of which may turn out to be highly pertinent. Your domestic bankers and brokers will rarely be able to handle any overseas ventures competently but, if they have an operation in the target country, they may well have a useful list of individual managers and analysts who follow equities from your home country.

Likewise, the big City law firms may claim extensive experience, but there is no substitute for a New York law firm if you want respect from US investment banks and funds – and several NY lawyers have London offices (try Cleary Gottlieb or Skadden Arps).

You should almost certainly take advice from local IR consultants in the target country, even if you do not wish to retain one. They will all be keen to have an 'exploratory' meeting and you can pick up many useful hints, and a good feel for the place, by discussing their experience of similar work.

The banks will have told you that they can handle everything and, if asked, will probably express disrespect for consultants, but an objective outsider to the deal can be invaluable. All banks have their regulars to pack the hall and impress you with the large audience, but the local consultancy should be able to add a well-researched list of contacts and to handle the (sometimes immense) job of inviting, checking and reminding invitees – and then keeping a list of actual attendees (which the bank will try to keep to itself) to form the basis of future invitation lists.

Your local operating managers will be a valuable addition to the hosting party but probably will not be suitable as day-to-day contacts in between your visits. So you may well need either a local full-time IR officer (ICI is said to spend £500,000 to maintain an IR operation in New York) or a consultant to maintain a list of interested investors, send them all major announcements and handle their queries – especially where differences in language or time-zone make your home office unsuitable.

On the other hand, every country has its clutch of PR consultants pretending to have pertinent IR experience. Check to see if their managers are local and then talk to *your* choice of two or three from their client list. Better still, the safest course – other than recommendations from other companies which got there before you – might be to try your favourite out by asking him to organize a small lunch or dinner with a few key investors, well before you get involved in roadshows, etc. See who he gets to come, and how well he's done his homework on your company.

IR societies are established in the USA, Canada, UK, France and Denmark and are being formed in most other major European countries. For example, the UK Investor Relations Society was formed in 1980, and comprises over 220 senior executives with management responsibility for IR, including CEOs, FDs, company secretaries and communications specialists. These societies and your opposite numbers in other companies will probably be able to give the best advice.

Organization – those irritating details

One area where you should certainly seek advice from locals or experienced outsiders is the whole range of practical organization, such as arranging hotels, travel, venues, presentation equipment, local language, jargon, etc.

The bank will undoubtedly tell you that it (or its favourite hotel) has ideal facilities; that local investors will not attend anywhere else; that investors want to hear the CEO speak, not watch videos or be distracted by slides; and that they will (or will not) understand your accounting methods and language. Don't listen! The first time you arrive to find no lectern, lights which cannot be dimmed, carousels which won't take your slides, no-one to take guests' names for your records, unsuitable rooms, and an audience who are not interested in European shares and think turnover refers to staff changes as opposed to revenue – and tell you admiringly about the multi-media show some company did last week – you'll wish you had not been so poorly advised!

Get yourself invited to a few presentations by local companies and gauge audience reactions if you really want to be sure. Even that may not be the best guide – UK privatization roadshows broke new ground in stage techniques in the USA, even compared to US IR shows – and the audiences loved them (and remembered them!).

While investors may not be prepared to travel too far for a presentation (unless it's something very special) they certainly get bored going to the same dull venue day after day and an unusual venue might actually persuade them to choose your presentation rather than the other alternatives that week – or day (The New York Society of Investment Analysts reckon there are over 20 major presentations per day in New York!). Montreal's Île Ste. Hélène, Amsterdam's maritime museum and Philadelphia's College of Physicians Museum (with its grisly exhibits) have all been used with great success. Even the Eiffel Tower and the galleries above Tower Bridge have been big hits – especially as most of the locals had never been up them!

Obviously, investor events can vary from one man in his office, through meetings with a dozen fund managers in one institution, to the major presentations with a hundred (or more) in the audience. Equally obviously, the audio-visual and lighting requirements will vary accordingly – from one annual report to a hundred full packs, microphones, multiple projectors and lighting trees, with flip charts or monitors in between.

Any equipment you need should be available locally, but it is usually a false economy to rely entirely on local people to set it up. For example, a presentation designed with slide back-up will fail to impress if there is no black-out available or the room is set out badly.

Unnecessary stress will reduce the team's performance and can be saved by sending one person ahead to check all preparations. If staff are in short supply, this can be an excellent perk for an inexperienced member of staff – if he has any doubts, he can at least call for help before panic becomes necessary.

Broadway show? – the presentation

The people of Zurich (and Frankfurt) are not as conservative as their bankers would have you believe – they particularly enjoy British humour in videos and commercials (if it's enunciated clearly enough). In most countries (except Japan and perhaps France) few people will use simultaneous translation equipment if you provide it (although some may be offended if you don't). They will mostly try to follow you in English, so you'll need at least a salutation in local language, to show some effort, plus a short script, slowly spoken, with key points repeated. Watch out for different meanings of words (like revenue and earnings) and for different ratios in use. You may want at least the headings translated on slides to prevent distraction, and you must check whether the locals know about the share purchase and dividend payment methods you'll be using, and the difference between your accounting policies and theirs.

Make sure your script addresses local concerns, fashions and ignorance. If they don't know your company, tell them who the local equivalent would be – and any international ones. Don't over-emphasize EPS if they're cashflow crazy. Reassure them that quarterly results are not normal in your country and that they will not be at a disadvantage to your domestic shareholders.

The Americans have exported their custom of eating before the presentation to many countries. But local investors – even in the USA! – often prefer to eat afterwards so that they have time to ask questions that your presentation did not address. However, they may be accustomed to arriving late, so your invitation letter should give the time the presentation will start.

There is no substitute for studying local newspapers and analysts' reports to see what investors' concerns are. Familiarize yourself with local competitors, customs and trading methods; talk to other companies or consultants with local experience, and then make sure your presentation addresses these issues.

Do they understand you?

Foreign investors frequently lack knowledge on issues you had never thought of addressing. A recent survey of US fund managers by Broadgate Consultants in the USA found that respondents often lack the basic information they need relating to the two reasons for owning equities – dividends and growth. Here are some of their findings:

Is the information on dividends on foreign stocks clear?

	per cent
Very clear	8
Somewhat clear	52
Not clear	34
Don't know	6

How well-informed are you on issues of corporate governance for the foreign firms in which you invest?

	per cent
Very well-informed	15
Somewhat informed	58
Uninformed	23
Don't know	4

US investors also complained that proxy material from foreign firms frequently arrived too late to permit them to vote.

Retrograde motion (flowback)

Many factors affect the flow of investment funds across national boundaries, on top of the ordinary fluctuations within the domestic market. These complicate the process of valuation of a foreign investment, and can result in massive volatility as large international funds move in and out of a share.

The most important outside factor is obviously currency fluctuation. Clearly, a US fund will be valuing its investments in dollars, so that a big change in dollar exchange rates might not only affect investors' views of a company's earning power because of the US proportion of its profits, but will also change the dollar value of the stock.

Overseas equity investment is used by many funds to hedge against currency and national economy risks, so that investors in one country may well all act together when either the exchange rate changes or news coverage in their media changes their view of a company's home country. If much of this investment is done by computer programmes, the resulting share price movements can be frighteningly fast.

Where smaller changes in exchange rates occur, ordinary investors may well ignore them, but this can leave a small differential between the domestic and foreign rates. In sophisticated markets (especially New York) there will be *arbitrageurs* who are prepared to buy large blocks of stock in the cheaper of the two markets and sell it in the other to realize this differential. Hence, shares can be sucked away from genuine investors and passed to short-term traders. The only way to prevent this trend is to continuously stimulate demand from genuine investors, so that a gap never opens up.

Unfortunately, stamp duty and other restrictions can act as something of a one-way valve between the two markets. For example, stamp duty reserve tax adds 1.5 per cent to the cost of UK shares taken abroad – an irritating disincentive on the outward movement of shares with no corresponding disincentive applying to shares flowing back into the UK.

Encouraging foreign investment, therefore, can be a little like pushing water up hill until the volume of trading in the foreign land creates a more independent market. Exchange rates, different accounting policies and reporting frequencies, and less contact with management, all tend to discourage the foreign investor, so that the flow of stock is likely to be back to the home country (flowback) unless the company works hard at encouraging demand at the other end.

In extreme cases – usually where greedy bankers have persuaded the company to issue more shares than there is a natural market for – flowback can be very high and very embarrassing. Indeed, the volume of shares returning to the home market may well depress the company's share price at home too. A good example was that of the Canadian bank, Toronto Dominion. It issued 4.5 million shares in Tokyo in May 1986; by March 1988 this was down to just over 700,000. Lonrho's experience was nearly as bad – 15 million shares down to three million in four months after its July 1987 Tokyo issue.

Flowback has been reported from many a US and European issue too. When British Telecom was marketed so hard (and sold so cheap) by the Government, UK demand pulled back virtually all of the shares issued in the USA. And when confidence in the luxury car market and in the US dollar slumped simultaneously, Jaguar's US equity base plummeted from 50 per cent to 20 per cent of the total, taking the price down with it!

But flowback in other markets is seldom to the degree that seems common in Japan (see Chapter 10). This is clearly a function of demand in the target markets and it is hard to forgive either the company or its advisers for the extreme examples. If there was so little demand for the shares in the short term, then the company has been given, and has accepted, poor advice in thinking there was more. And if there is no longer-term market, the company has failed to stimulate demand through its IR programme. In both cases, the programme was misconceived, poorly planned, ill-prepared or pathetically executed – or all four. Plenty of companies have succeeded in establishing successful overseas markets, so it can be done.

Costs and benefits – is it all worth it?

Any consideration of overseas listings, then, should start with a decision on the company's objectives. You can probably achieve many of them without leaving the home country. Many more are probably achievable through an active IR programme in each key overseas market. But if you do decide on listings, it is going to be costly (in terms of both money and executive time); it is not going to generate substantial share trading volume in the short term; and it is going to involve a permanent increase in accounting, legal and IR complexity. So it should not be undertaken lightly. There needs to be an honest evaluation of the costs and potential benefits to the company – as opposed to its bankers, lawyers, accountants and other consultants – and of the senior management team's commitment to making it work.

- Accountancy costs to prepare accounts under different Generally Accepted Accounting Principles (GAAP) for each country. For an Amsterdam listing, the additional requirements are negligible; for New York or Tokyo, they may take an army of accountants up to two years to prepare! They require a completely different calculation of profit performance for the last five years (including all acquired companies), different treatment of balance sheet, tax and transaction figures, and the presentation of considerably more segmental analysis (eg, asset and capital allocation).
- Legal costs to prepare a prospectus, dealing agreements and many other documents, sometimes in a foreign language (arguably, always in a foreign language since US legal jargon bears little similarity to English). Then there may be lengthy 'due diligence' sessions for teams of lawyers acting for you and for the banks to satisfy themselves, through interrogation of top financial and line managers, that the documentation is an accurate description of the securities involved.
- Audit fees to have all of the above separately audited.
- Transaction fees. If any new shares are to be issued, these are generally a few per cent of the proceeds. If not, they will be a flat fee. Both are negotiable and can vary widely. Ask for lists of recent fees for other listings – in most countries they have to be shown in

the prospectus, so the bank will be able to give you a table, although the stated figures rarely represent the full total.

- Marketing costs for the IR roadshow, PR and IR consultants, equipment hire and set-up (projectors, etc), travel, hotels, venues and food, brochures, gifts (almost mandatory in Japan), etc.
- Printing costs of prospectuses, other documents and brochures, and possibly of ADR certificates, etc.
- Continuing obligation costs. Accounting, legal and audit fees will be charged each year for any separate report required (eg, form 20F in the USA, which is the foreign company equivalent of form 10K, the 'official' annual report for the regulatory authorities). Results advertising will certainly be desirable and is mandatory in some countries (such as France, where every company announcement must be published as an advertisement, in leading newspapers). Banks, depositories and other agents will charge annual fees. You may need local consultancies, or even a local IR office. There will be a need for at least one 'roadshow' every year.

In reality, the total launch cost will vary from about £10,000 for a simple listing in Amsterdam to £250,000 or more for a share issue in Tokyo.

The benefits will rarely be immediate (except for the proceeds of an issue) and may not be achieved at all if the company fails to keep up the IR effort – indeed you could end up looking very stupid. It can also be argued that harmonization of regulations and accounting standards will create a global market where multiple listings become unnecessary, but this is a distant and uncertain prospect. In the meantime, those companies that list in foreign countries with well-considered objectives and well-planned and executed IR programmes often achieve considerable gains. Some, like Glaxo and ADT, might say that they have achieved an upward re-rating too.

New issue or simple listing

As we have said, it is worth bearing in mind that limited objectives may well be achievable without a listing or an issue. Many companies have achieved considerable increased overseas investment in their shares through well-planned and executed IR programmes, without ever listing or issuing shares. In fact, the first step in the consideration phase should almost certainly be IR visits and roadshows to evaluate the market's reaction, the skills and commitment of the bankers and other advisers and – perhaps above all – to expose the management team to the traumatic experience as a test of their commitment!

But if you have seriously committed yourself to any of the objectives we have discussed, a listing will probably be necessary at some stage. The difficulty is that stimulating the market from scratch can be an arduous process. If time is on your side, a gradual build-up is likely to prove much more stable – and economic.

There is no doubt – as greedy bankers will be sure to point out – that an issue of new shares will generate trading activity much more quickly than a simple listing, although, as we have seen, you need to guard against it all being one way. It's interesting to note how the extra fees from an issue can concentrate the minds of the bankers on doing a good job and on motivating their sales forces.

An issue will probably also involve a large underwriting or sub-management group, too, so it will immediately raise your profile with other key securities firms, as well as with the Press. Chinese walls may be bent a little too – corporate finance teams in major houses dare not promise favourable research coverage, but they can usually arrange for you to meet that key analyst who has resisted previous invitations.

Remember, however, that a share issue will almost certainly involve a higher level of regulatory complexity (see Chapter 9), and a poor IR plan will be much more publicly exposed. If the eventual intention is to issue shares actively in the foreign market, these procedures will be inevitable. But the company must carefully weigh the benefits of a quicker establishment of a liquid market, and getting the pain of issue registration behind it, against the longer, but easier and cheaper, gradualist approach.

Going for it – but where?

If you have convinced yourself – and your colleagues – that you should go ahead with an overseas programme, how do you decide where to start? In some cases, the company will only have operations and financial programmes in one overseas area, so the decision is easy. Others operate worldwide and may have more difficult decisions to make.

So internal factors will be the first priority and, of course, the objectives which are driving the push into foreign markets. But some understanding of the principal security markets will help in deciding priorities.

A book could be written on each of the principal markets (Japan, the USA and Europe) – indeed there are several such books on the US market, and several organizations have produced guides to the Japanese and European security markets. Detailed advice is beyond the scope of this book, so the following is simply an overview, with summaries in the next three chapters.

We have already seen that Japan is the largest market, at about a third of the world total market (although Chapter 9 shows that this is largely an illusion). The USA is second largest, at just over a quarter of the world market and Europe is close behind at a quarter – a third of it in the UK alone.

Tokyo is also by far the most expensive market to list on and has only achieved prominence very recently. No surprise, then, that only 161 foreign companies have listed there. By contrast, 387 have listed on the three US exchanges and about 300 foreign companies have 1,059 listings on the various European exchanges – 201 in London alone. But in foreign equity investment, even in post-crash 1988, Japan already reached levels exceeding $91 billion in bonds, and almost $3 billion in stocks – and clearly will remain a major world force.

Tokyo has also been the best performing of the major exchanges around the world since 1960, at 12.25 per cent compound. The UK was number two at 8.6 per cent, followed closely by the USA, and then Canada and the other European markets. To give a sense of perspective, though, it's worth mentioning that some of the smaller world markets out-performed all of these, particularly in the last four years. Believe it or not, the top performer was the Philippines. And Korea, Zimbabwe, Taiwan, Chile and Mexico all out-performed Tokyo!

We have also seen that Japan tends to have the highest flowback rates, and in Chapter 9 we argue that the Japanese are only active foreign investors through foreign markets. So we would leave Japan to those companies which are looking for more than prime investment from their foreign IR – ie those with existing or intended operations in the region.

The USA is genuinely the largest equity market – and the most volatile and geographically dispersed (see Chapter 8). US investors channelled $1.9 billion into foreign equities in 1988, $1.2 billion of it into Europe. The 387 foreign companies already listed in the USA alone raised $1.3 billion there in 1988.

The US market has excellent resources, too, in terms of financial and IR advice. Its market has grown consistently and continues to do so. And the USA still accounts for many more European acquisitions than Europe does, so it should remain a major trading, financial and operational partner for many years to come.

Europe cannot yet be considered to be one market, although it could be argued that there are more cities important to an IR programme in the USA than in Europe. Language, custom and regulatory differences complicate the IR role, but, as we argue in Chapter 10, European companies may have less choice about the need for an IR programme here than anywhere else – in the securities markets, many of the changes will take place *before* 1992.

These, then, are the main markets. Hong Kong, Singapore, Sydney,

Toronto and Johannesburg are important only to companies which operate there, as are the remaining exchanges in the third league.

CHAPTER 8

Two countries divided by a common language
– the US market, still the world's greatest opportunity?

'Since you took us over, several of my managers have tried to buy shares, but the local brokers can't find them! They say BET on the big board is Bethlehem Corp – and has been for 55 years. The only other BET they've heard of is Black Entertainment Television. Can't we buy your shares here?'

For the world's largest capitalist market, the USA can often turn out to be a remarkably parochial place. Less than three per cent of the population has ever travelled abroad. Of the remainder, many have never left their home state – and they regard a Wall Street scandal as international news.

The US securities markets, then, may be the most sophisticated in the world – but they are also the most spread out and they cover many areas where the typical fund manager feels brave if he buys shares in a company based just a few miles away over the Canadian border.

The world's largest funds

In terms of institutional investment, the top ten cities in North America account for 60 per cent of the funds under management, and although New York and Boston are much larger than the remainder, no serious IR programme can afford to ignore cities like Chicago, Los Angeles, San Francisco and Philadelphia.

As we have already said, the US pension funds have so far only invested five per cent of their funds in foreign equities (even though the 'prudent man rule' has permitted ten per cent since 1974) and 65 per cent of these investments are managed through offshore offices. But over half of the $1 billion-plus funds had reached ten per cent by 1988, and many of the insurance companies and investment trusts have much higher proportions invested abroad. Furthermore, the truly huge companies like Fidelity are managing international portfolios for major investors all over the world.

Highly active private investors

Individual investors – the so-called 'retail' market in the USA – still account for $700–800 billion. And they are served by about 68,000 registered retail brokers who are even more spread out across this vast country, so the truly determined IR manager in a US company may well be visiting over 50 cities a year. There is some overlap with the institutional concentration but the top ten cities only account for 30 per cent of the available funds.

Few foreign companies can afford to match their US counterparts' efforts in retail IR, but a carefully planned programme can certainly pay off since US retail investors trade each of their stocks less than a quarter as often as US institutions. When BET decided to issue shares in the USA, it was determined not to dilute its unusually high proportion of individual shareholdings. For two years ahead of the issue, senior managers called on local retail brokers whenever they visited operations or institutions in the USA, and Merrill Lynch was brought in as co-manager with Goldman Sachs (see Assembling your team, page 133). As a result, 65 per cent of the $110 million issue was bought by retail investors – and the flowback following Black Monday (unluckily only three months after the issue) was much less than most other foreign companies experienced.

ADR – American Discrimination Register?

Foreign shares cannot be directly traded in the USA and a highly sophisticated system has thus been developed for indirect trading. This is generally known as the ADR market, owing to the instrument involved – the American Depository Receipt. The security which is actually traded is an American Depository Share (ADS) – the ADR is simply the receipt showing how many ADSs the investor has bought.

To add to the confusion, an ADS does not necessarily equate directly with the shares it represents. Since US investors are accustomed to domestic companies' shares trading at $10–25 rather than the $3–5 which many European shares would cost, many companies aggregate their shares, making one ADS represent two, four or even ten ordinary shares.

If a US (or Canadian) investor wishes to buy any foreign shares for ownership in the USA, his broker can purchase them on their home exchanges and deposit them with a US bank under a legal depository agreement. The bank would then issue an ADR for these shares and keep a record of any subsequent changes of ownership. In practice, this would be prohibitively expensive for the broker or investor, unless the broker intended to establish a large, active market in the company's shares – in which case the company might be alarmed at having no access to the depository register.

For this reason, most companies which wish to develop an active US market in their shares – or find one has already developed – decide to control the market by sponsoring their ADR programme. They then pay the legal and launch fees for the depository agreement and the fee for distributing annual reports, dividends, etc. These sponsored ADRs can then be traded 'over-the-counter' by US brokers, and an IR programme can begin to establish a market.

However, any foreign company which wishes to achieve the objectives we have discussed is eventually going to want its ADRs quoted on one of the stock exchanges so that the dollar price is displayed on the exchange and in local newspapers and databases. At this stage, stock exchange listing rules and SEC (Securities and Exchanges Commission) registration will be involved. These are big steps and should not be taken lightly, but the shares cannot be used in acquisitions or employee share schemes without them.

The ADR market – going up?

Despite all the costs and complications, the ADR market has grown steadily since 1983 to a total of 782 ADR programmes in 1988, of which nearly 400 are listed. Annual ADR trading volumes grew rapidly up to 1987 and the drop in post-crash 1988 was not really dramatic – hardly surprising, as the leading ADR index performed twice as well as the main domestic share indices. New capital raised through ADR issues had grown dramatically in 1987 but note that 1988 was still above pre-1987 levels.

There is almost no doubt that this growth will continue. The performance of funds with high proportions of foreign investment has been much better than the rest, even in dollar terms, and US investors are rapidly recognizing the vulnerability their parochialism brings – particularly if they wish to win contracts to manage new funds against stiffening international competition.

On the other hand, it may take some time for your shares to reach decent levels of trading volume – depending on how well-known and active (in the USA) the company is and how effective an IR programme you establish. Bear in mind that a large US fund will not usually find it worthwhile to buy a small number of shares. But a large block may make them vulnerable if selling it would take up your entire ADR volume for several days.

In the early stages, then, you will need to find long-term funds or individual investors to build up the market liquidity. In the meantime, though, your higher visibility, your IR visits to them, and their ability to monitor your progress, may well result in large US funds increasing their holdings of your ordinary shares through your home market.

Regulatory barriers

US securities laws and regulations are amongst the toughest in the world and we all know how popular litigation is in the US.

The SEC no longer requires quarterly reports from foreign listed companies, but it does require the filing of 20F annual returns within 180 days of the year end, with considerably more detail than European annual reports normally contain. The main stock exchanges, too, impose differing levels of additional requirements – the New York Stock Exchange being the toughest – but none of these are too arduous for sizeable companies.

It is when issuing new shares, though, that companies will find the most extreme differences in the US market. US security law was apparently designed to protect private investors from the worst excesses of capitalism, but one could be forgiven for feeling that it has become counter-productive, in that the large company which dare not cut any corners ends up hiding its light under legal bushels whilst the cowboys sell their issues hard. If you asked a lawyer to sell your car for you he'd probably be sure to warn prospective buyers of any faults but he would be unlikely to give them an accurate idea of what a bargain it was!

In the States, if your share price dropped by a few cents following an issue, dozens of hungry lawyers would probably be combing the prospectus (form F1) for any unprovable claim or unmentioned risk and then persuading all those who bought the shares to join a class action against you. So Sid would have been illegal, but if he had been quoted in the prospectus he would have described in excruciating detail the immense risks involved in producing and distributing explosive and poisonous gases, the likelihood of a future government re-nationalizing British Gas at minimum compensation levels, and probably the fact that the chairman at the time was liable to unpredictable bouts of insulting investment analysts. He may even have mentioned that the

Will you be allocating a greater amount of your funds to overseas investment over the next five years?

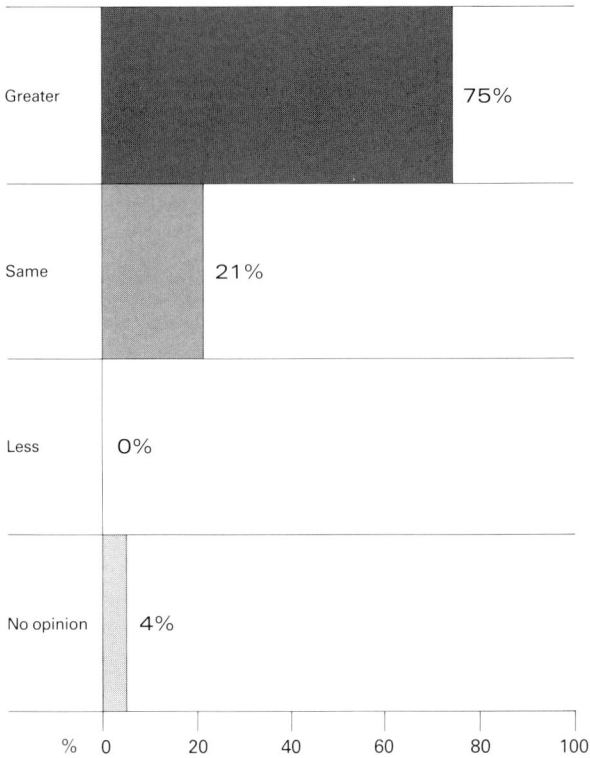

Greater — 75%

Same — 21%

Less — 0%

No opinion — 4%

% 0   20   40   60   80   100

Source: Broadgate Consultants, 1989 survey of leading US institutional investors

Figure 4

inflatable stage set used on the roadshow could explode, with catastrophic consequences. And the legal discussion over where the commas should go in all these dire warnings would have cost a fortune.

Once you have decided to do a US issue, you must consider yourself to be 'in registration' with the SEC, which means that the most draconian limitations apply. These prevent you from any publicity beyond your normal past practice in the USA (all the more reason to establish a reasonably high IR profile for a year or two beforehand) or any other action which could be interpreted by the SEC as being aimed at 'hyping' the issue. For a little-known company with no prior IR programme, therefore, the issue will be entirely at the mercy of the lead manager – your IR team will be severely limited.

This complexity is due to the fact that the first issue of shares in the USA by a foreign company counts as an Initial Public Offering (IPO), as if it was yet another undertaker or software house going public for the first time. The company's public quote for 300 years in London or Paris will be ignored – which is another classic example of US parochialism, which one can only hope the global market will trample over eventually.

Once the company has filed for an IPO and reported a few times on form 20F, however, registering further issues becomes very much simpler and quicker, yet again begging the question of whether you might as well jump all the hurdles at the beginning.

Assembling your team

Your US debut, then – whether listing or issue – will require an army of helpers, and the selection process can be a valuable learning period if you make sure you speak to the key players in each field.

The company will need a depository to hold the shares, issue ADRs, keep a register and distribute dividends and reports, etc. Since the Bank of New York acquired Irving Trust, they are now by far the biggest specialist in this field, with Morgan Guaranty trailing them. Both have European offices which can give valuable advice.

London printers can advise on suitable New York financial printers, but quiz them carefully over claimed abilities to link their systems so that the prospectus can be run from your head office but printed in New York.

Your chosen US bank and your domestic legal advisers can best advise on US law firms – they are all a pain in the neck and operate in teams of regiment size, but this is one field where you cannot do without a New York-based firm. (See also What value good advice, page 117.)

The choice of banks will depend on many factors, including existing relationships, and it is not possible here to give comprehensive advice. Of the largest, Goldman Sachs stands out for its arrogance as well as for its policy of never taking part in a hostile bid (except as defender – for which it has a good reputation). Little generalization can be made about the others except that some are almost wholly involved with institutions (Morgan Stanley, First Boston), whereas others have strong retail chains to service private investors (Merrill Lynch, Shearson Lehman).

The major PR consultancies mostly have operations, or at least affiliations, on both sides of the Atlantic but, once again, make them prove any claim they make to have transatlantic IR experience: ask them for a list of clients for whom they consult, on both sides of the pond.

In the more specialized IR field, Valin Pollen owns Carter in New York and City & Commercial shares parents with Georgeson. Both are highly-respected in US IR circles, as are Taylor Rafferty (linked with London's Makinson Cowell) and Broadgate (linked with London's Blackwood Financial Communications).

Exchanging partners – which stock exchange to choose

As most of us are only too aware – since they each have hungry sales teams here in London – there are three major stock exchanges in the USA. The granddaddy of them all, of course, is the New York Stock Exchange, better known as the NYSE or 'The BIG Board'. The NYSE is still the biggest exchange with 1,681 companies listed on it, representing a market capitalization of $2.5 trillion. It still operates on the traditional 'open outcry' trading floor principle like London in the good old days, except that each stock is handled by one 'specialist' rather than several jobbers.

Critics would say that the system is slower, more expensive and less efficient than the electronic system of competing market-makers that London now uses, but fans point to the enormous value of having one man who knows everything there is to know about the market for that stock and who can use his own book to smooth out fluctuations. The Big Board still dominates trading in blue-chip stocks and many investors will only invest in NYSE stocks.

The London electronic system, of course, was basically copied from the second largest US exchange, NASDAQ – the National Association of Security Dealers Automated Quotation System – with 4,235 companies listed and a market value of $339 billion. Started in the 1950s as an over-the-counter market, it attracted many of the high-flying growth stocks and – they grew!

The third market is the American Stock Exchange, another open outcry trading floor with specialists. Known as 'the Curb', it started in the 18th Century to handle secondary stocks. It has been decisively overtaken by NASDAQ and has a value of $112 billion with 896 companies listed. It is apparently moving towards specialization in traded options and other instruments. BAT is the only major UK company listed there and the value of its ADR volume is tiny.

NASDAQ, by contrast, has attracted the largest number of foreign listings, with 270, and its 1988 ADR volume was worth almost $10 billion. Since UK companies, no matter what their size, are basically new stocks to the US when they first list, NASDAQ has appealed to many of them as the natural exchange, and its listing requirements and fees are substantially less than those of The Big Board.

The NYSE, then, has a total of 77 foreign listings – but its ADR volume is *worth* three times as much as the other two put together. Its blue-chip, stable, prestigious image might be more suitable for some companies than the more glamorous, volatile image of NASDAQ, but it is more expensive and both have their strengths. The NYSE has one advantage, however: the CEO can visit, have his picture taken and receive a very handsome trophy of a bull and bear locked in a dubious embrace!

Born in the USA

Investor relations had its origins in the USA, and many US companies have highly sophisticated IR programmes run by IR vice presidents. One result is that analysts and fund managers will always have plenty of alternatives to a meeting with you. More than anywhere else, you will be in a competitive environment and will have to give them good value if you want to sell to them. Still, the team with a well-planned presentation need have no fears: the average US domestic effort is surprisingly poor.

Whichever route you choose, one of the first tasks will be to persuade a few of the key analysts in the sector to start research coverage on your company. The US version of Big Bang resulted in a huge reduction in sell-side (broker's) analysts and increase in buy-side (institutional) analysts, but the sell-side analysts who survived often have enormous influence, particularly those working in houses with big retail sales forces.

Plotting the key institutional concentrations, retail investment centres (if you aim to appeal to them) and your own operations will show what the priorities should be and which analysts will help most (a regional broker may well have a relevant specialist who is well-respected but less sought-after than those in the major houses).

The word roadshow also originated in the USA and is very apt; even if the typical US company does it badly, they are used to having to plan hectic series of meetings. To make the transatlantic trip worthwhile and to meet the key players at least once a year, the top team (almost certainly including the CEO and CFO) will probably need to plan *at least* two one-week trips per year, visiting four or five cities each time. Planning a big lunchtime show, a few one-on-one meetings and a dinner every day, plus an air trip and change of hotels, makes the average pop group's schedule look like a picnic.

A private jet may well be necessary to avoid airline schedules' mismatch with yours and to obviate the need for queues, advance check-

Rate the issues of greatest concern

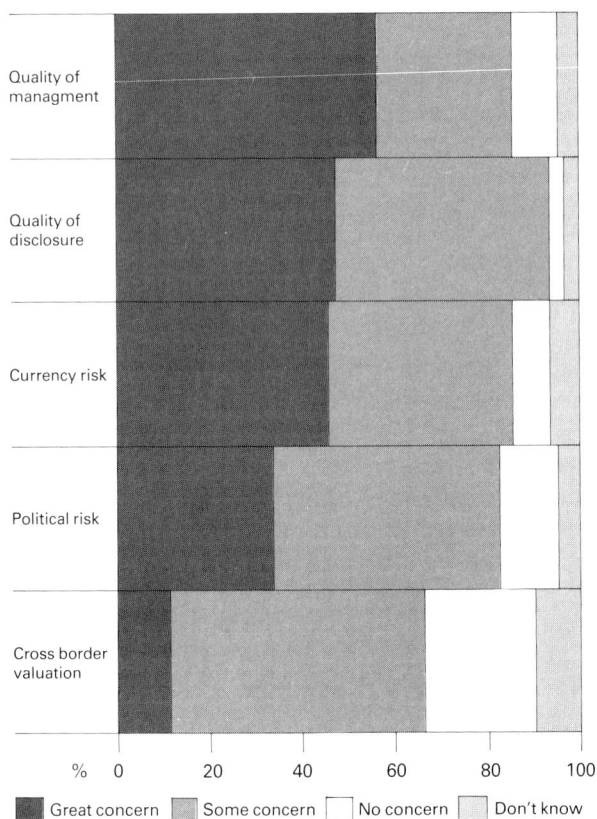

Source: Broadgate Consultants, 1989 survey of leading US institutional investors

Figure 5

in and slow passenger loading. And, as elsewhere, a support team who can travel ahead, handle your check-in at hotels, and set up and check equipment, etc, will be a near-essential.

We have already covered the more general hints in Chapter 7 but there are a few more details peculiar (literally) to the US market.

One is the prevalence of electronic databases. This homeland of the computer can offer a wealth of information at the touch of a button and an IR manager ignores them at his peril. For planning purposes, there are two vital services. Institutions in the USA are obliged to file a quarterly return on form 13F, summarizing their investment policies and listing their main investments. Not surprisingly, a number of services have sprung up to turn this valuable data into invaluable

What is the primary reason you invest in foreign equities?

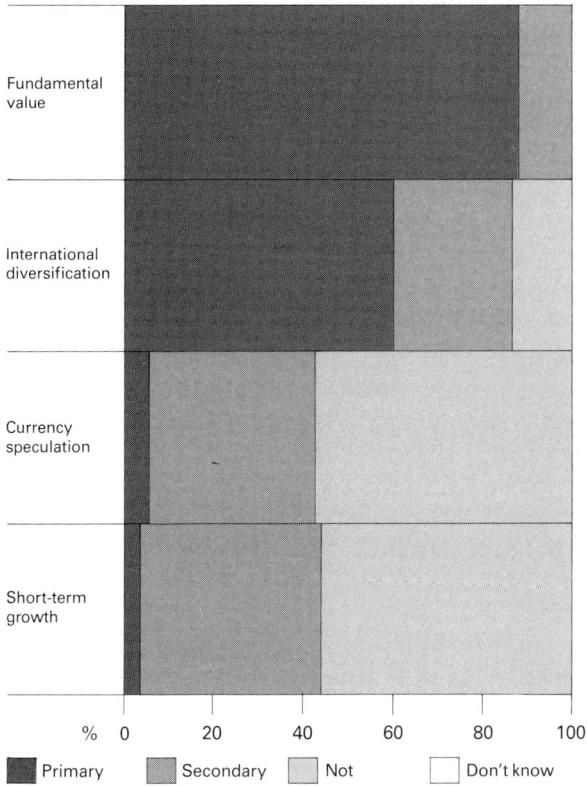

Source: Broadgate Consultants, 1989 survey of leading US institutional investors

Figure 6

databases. From such 13F services, you can feed in your company's yield, PER, cash flow and asset features, etc, and obtain a list of funds whose investment criteria you meet. Or you can feed in a list of companies you feel are similar to yours and see which funds own their shares.

The best-known service in this area is from Technimetrics, whose strong point is their comprehensive database of names of contacts – from chief executives in funds to analysts covering each sector. They can provide mailing labels, print-outs, computer discs, etc.

Similarly, several companies – notably Valueline – have databases which show the vital statistics of listed companies and are relied on by retail brokers and investors; so persuading them to add your company will probably be more effective than several dozen presentations in dusty mid-West towns.

The International Brokers Estimate System (IBES) shows analysts estimates for you and your chosen list of peer companies with comparison of historic and expected earnings, PER, yield, etc – very helpful in choosing your strong and weak points.

Since there is no section 212 of the Companies Act in the USA, identifying beneficial owners of the company's stock is a very different exercise. The SEC has made brokers ask their clients whether or not they are prepared to be exposed and you can get a list – at a price – of Non-Objecting Beneficial Owners (known by the delightful acronym 'NOBOs') from registrars, if you are a domestic company, and from depository agents, if you are a foreign company.

A further stage is possible largely as a result of stricter enforcement of proxy voting in the States. Companies are obliged in certain circumstances to obtain proxy forms from a minimum percentage of shareholders, and a whole specialist industry exists to track down, and obtain votes from, shareholders – 'proxy solicitation'. Because these firms have worked through so many companies' share registers, they can often identify many of the OBOs (Objecting Beneficial Owners) from their account numbers, code names, etc.

Conclusion

The complexities of this market defy brief description – and can all too easily cause insomnia, if not nervous breakdown! But it should be pointed out that problems usually create opportunities. The emerging US appetite for foreign investment is still largely unsatisfied. Very few foreign companies are seriously competing for this huge pool of dollars and those that have proper IR programmes generally find their efforts well rewarded. If the top team are willing to spend at least two exhausting weeks on the road each year and to pay for lower-level representation in between, the US market could well take the driver's seat for your shares, as it has in the past for Jaguar, Glaxo, Hanson, Saatchi, ADT and others.

1988 saw LEP Group become the first to make a US acquisition entirely for ADRs (although BP's 1987 purchase of Standard Oil, and many other mergers, had used ADRs for at least part of the consideration) and BET became the first to create an ADR ESOP. The rate of European acquisitions in the USA, and the US enthusiasm for European equities guarantees that this will remain amongst the favourite targets for overseas IR.

CHAPTER 9

Sunrise or sunset?
– *Japan, immature giant?*

The roar of laughter from the room full of Japanese fund managers, as the CEO started the final part of his presentation – a highly favourable assessment of his company's advantage over its Japanese competitors – brought him to a shocked standstill, from which he took long seconds to recover. Only after the show, when the guests had left, could the sponsoring Japanese banker convince him that it was his dig at the key US competitor which had caused their mirth – the delay was simply the result of the interpreter trailing nearly a minute behind his speech!

Radically different customs and regulations – to say nothing of language and share ratings – are enough to confound any chief executive. And costs of up to a quarter of a million pounds for a Tokyo listing – not to mention hotel room rates – certainly confound most CFOs.

These costs (and NatWest is said to have incurred £5 million in fees and commission only, for its £100 million issue) have not deterred some brave souls from launching their shares on the Tokyo Stock Exchange (TSE). Over 100 foreign companies are listed on the TSE's Foreign Section, compared with just 11 in 1984, with trading volume multiplying 150 times during those five years. The reason? No doubt it has something to do with the size of the Japanese market – now more than 50 per cent bigger than the USA and accounting for a third of the world equity market. Or the staggering increases in Japanese investment in foreign equities – over $12.6 billion in 1987 alone.

Is Tokyo really the biggest and best?

Yet much of this is hype and illusion – if not manipulation. Probably two thirds of all equity in Japanese firms is tied up in cross-holdings by other corporations or banks. Hence the remaining shares have a scarcity value which enhances their price – and the apparent size of the market. If we exclude these shares – which are virtually never traded – Tokyo falls behind both the USA and Europe in terms of market capitalization.

And the TSE is not the fastest-growing market – according to the International Finance Corporation, between the ends of 1984 and 1988, the Philippines, Korea, Zimbabwe, Taiwan, Chile and Mexico all out-performed it! There have been accusations that the very thin market for shares on the TSE allows the big securities houses to move the whole market, and that politically-inspired manipulation has been used to create an impression of strength which is not real. The *Asian Wall Street Journal* noted that the last trading day of 1987 saw massive intervention by the top firms which reversed a decline that would have left the post-crash TSE looking worse than either London or New York.

Foreign trading volume

And, while the Japanese have certainly been buying foreign stocks, they have been doing so through other markets – the TSE's Foreign Section has recorded little growth since the end of 1985 and nearly half of the volume of trade since then has been in one issue – Telefonica. Trading on the Foreign Section took off, mysteriously, early in 1985 (volume of 31.7 million shares in the first half compared with 4.5 million in the whole of 1984). It may have reached 750 million shares in 1987 but its post-crash quarterly trading volume has remained below 1986's peak. Foreign listings accelerated immediately the 1985 surge occurred – ten in the second half of that year and around 30 per year since, giving the current total of over 100.

None of this need deter the company which understands what it is getting into. TSE volume may be nothing to write home about but that is largely because transaction costs – after three recent reductions – are twice those of the NYSE. And, as with other overseas listings, it may well turn out that companies which list in Tokyo will attract more Japanese investment through their home market.

The Tokyo market

Foreign stocks listed in Tokyo are recorded by receipts issued by the Japan Securities Clearing Corp (JSCC). The number of shares retained after flowback (see page 121) is usually small, although this is not the only measurement of the effectiveness of a listing (see page 107).

Japan has no large, liquid market for over-the-counter unlisted shares, like that in the USA, so there is nowhere for demand and liquidity in a company's stock to build-up ahead of a full listing.

Cable & Wireless sold 8 million shares there in 1985 and 30,000 Japanese investors bought British Telecom shares in the same year's privatization. Yet Cable & Wireless became the first British TSE listing in April 1986, followed by BT. Both companies found the local over-the-counter market unable to cope with the needs of investors for a liquid market.

Hurdles to jump

Companies have no choice, then, but to proceed directly to a full listing if they feel that simpler IR programmes are inadequate. And here they meet a Catch 22 of magnificent simplicity: in order to be listed on the TSE, they must first prove that they have, already, a minimum of 1,000 Japanese shareholders. This is likely to be very hard to achieve from an IR programme alone and gives suspiciously strong backing to the entreaties of the Japanese banks that you launch your shares through an issue (or a series of them). To suggest that this is a conspiracy between officials and bankers would seem paranoid in any country less renowned for its government / bank cosiness.

Accounting, legal and marketing costs and complexities will add to the difficulties in justifying a TSE listing. Japanese Generally Accepted Accounting Principles (GAAP) require accounts which bear little resemblance to their domestic parents. In particular, Japanese companies are not required to consolidate all subsidiaries, which again distorts their price / earnings – their real earnings are usually much higher than stated – and this difference probably accounts for most of the PER differential which is not explained by the very thin market.

Legal and translation costs will also be high, since experts are much more scarce than for other overseas markets, and hotel and entertainment costs are staggering to the European visitor.

Where to turn for advice

If sensible commercial objectives apply, the major Japanese banks – Nomura, Daiwa, Yamaichi and Nikko – will be eager to advise on procedures, time-scales, costs, etc. As with any foreign listing, it may well be sensible to spend a year or two on establishing an IR programme before taking the plunge (although the banks will often try to discourage such delays!) and it certainly pays to study cost estimates carefully for omissions.

There is no well-established IR society in Tokyo but the British IRS has several members who have trodden the Japanese path. IR Japan is probably the leading consultancy and has a wealth of useful information. Other international consultancies have cashed in on the rush for Tokyo – amongst them Dewe Rogerson, Gavin Anderson, and Burson Marsteller.

If other objectives do not apply – now or in the near future – and you are looking only for more Japanese investment, it may well make sense to establish a professional IR programme and forget the listing – at least until the TSE matures. Increasing numbers of foreign companies do roadshows in Japan – which will certainly take up a working week – and report growing Japanese representation on their share registers.

Is the demand there?

Some of the leading bankers, Japanese and international, consider this essential for any aspiring global stock (which may have something to do with their share of the still considerable cost – not to mention their perpetual love of league tables showing how many such exercises they have sponsored!).

But some of the top Japanese banks argue that it is not the first step. They point out that Japanese individuals may appear to have high savings ratios, but that these are declining and equity investment is not a high proportion of them. In particular, investment in foreign equities is usually restricted to only the companies best known in Japan – like IBM, Walt Disney and Glaxo. Certainly the willingness of Japanese individuals to buy shares shortly after the 1987 crash in those companies which had been listed on the TSE for some time was an encouraging sign.

Moreover, the institutions which *are* investing huge amounts overseas (whilst many have a strong preference for bonds and ultra-high yield stocks) usually do so through overseas offices. So it probably makes sense for companies to mount presentations for Japanese fund managers on their home ground until they start to see real interest growing.

It may well be best to do these separately from other presentations, since the Japanese investor will probably have different criteria from most. He tends to be income-orientated and risk averse, and his ability to judge managers of foreign firms quickly is poor, so he will often be more comfortable if he receives separate attention.

Saatchi, NatWest, Fisons and GKN are amongst other UK companies to have issued shares in Tokyo. All have achieved their issues at close to the prevailing London price – although militant UK institutions argue that this ignores the costs of the issue and the earlier drop in the share price when the issue was first announced. (For the company, which gets to keep a much higher proportion of the proceeds than it would in a deeply discounted rights issue, this may sound like dog-in-the-manger language.)

One of the problems yet to be totally overcome with the Japanese issues is that of flowback (see Retrograde motion (flowback), page 121). TSE issues appear to have the world's worst record in this area and several companies (usually those that had no objectives besides raising 'cheap' funds – reinforcing the argument we have already made) have ended up wondering whether the proceeds of the issue were sufficient justification for the massive cost and effort and for the anger of their existing shareholders.

A sustained commitment to an IR programme can certainly bring success from a TSE listing (as Glaxo has proved). But the immaturity of the Japanese market in equity investment generally, and foreign equity investment particularly, should deter any CEO who has not set himself clear and well-evaluated objectives or is not prepared to commit himself to considerable and continuous suffering and expense!

CHAPTER 10

French connection or Italian job?
– *continental Europe, underestimated embryo?*

'Well, it will be difficult to explain to our clients why we have put your shares in his portfolio – you're not exactly an IBM or a Phillip Morris are you?'

Is there any point in trying to reach continental investors? And does the Swiss banker actually expect to have to justify his decisions to his Sicilian clients or is he softening you up for a bigger fee or trying to deter you altogether?

The European stock exchanges collectively make up about a quarter of the world equity market. While London accounts for a third of this total, the EEC security markets threaten to become more unified than ever before during the next decade – and, just possibly, by 1992. With 320 million people arguably likely to take equity investment more seriously – and certainly becoming sophisticated enough, and regulated enough, to take pensions and insurance more seriously – the creation of a single market could produce changes in the securities market which would dwarf the recent emergence of Japan.

Harmonization growing

Even if Europe continues its tradition of in-fighting, the imposition of some overall regulations of the EEC security markets is already underway and the IR implications of this should not be under-estimated. EEC listing requirements already apply and, with agreement reached on lifting exchange controls throughout the EEC, banks, stock exchanges and governments are manoeuvring to anticipate fairly immediate, and vast, flows of funds between their countries. Withholding taxes, transaction costs, offering and listing requirements, accounting policies and many of the other artificial constraints that have traditionally limited the freedom of investors and lenders have suddenly come under intense pressure.

When Nestlé bid for Rowntree in 1988, it set off a bandwagon of complaints over reciprocity of vulnerability that threatens to sweep away many more barriers to financial trading. Indeed, Nestlé led what is likely to be a tortoise-like rush to abandon the two-tier share structure which makes Swiss companies almost unassailable (and therefore unpopular as predators) by restructuring its equity in December 1988. By April 1989, 20 per cent of its voting shares had already been bought by foreigners. (Switzerland, of course, is outside the EEC, but its importance as a centre for international capital management makes it imperative for consideration alongside other European markets.)

Many years are likely to pass before the EEC can be treated as a homogeneous equity market – if it ever can! German companies – like those in Japan – have traditionally been funded, and largely owned, by banks, and have only very recently shown signs of emerging onto the global equity markets. Various types of institution in several European countries live with official limits on overseas investment and traditional attitudes may survive longer than these official barriers.

Currently, few European funds would have more than five per cent of their funds under management invested in foreign equities. A typical portfolio might be illustrated by one Dutch fund, which has: 1.2 per cent invested in US equity, 0.7 per cent in Japanese, 0.3 per cent in West German, 0.2 per cent in British and 0.1 per cent in Australian, Swiss, French and Canadian shares. Michael Howell of Salomon Brothers' European equity research desk calculates that continental investment flows into the UK alone in 1987 totalled $44 billion. But, of course, these flows vary enormously.

Likewise, those companies which set themselves realistic IR objectives and pursue them with determination and consistency could transform their share registers and their funding options.

Investment constraints on European investors

European countries impose many restrictions on how much institutional investors can invest in foreign equities. *Investor Relations*, Spring 1989, gives the following summary of restrictions (but note that locally-listed companies are often *not* classified as foreign):

France

Pension funds
Only 50 per cent of a total portfolio invested in foreign equities, which must be equities listed on major overseas exchanges.

Insurance companies
No restriction provided foreign equity is listed on the Paris Bourse. Guidelines call for 'diligent distribution'.

West Germany

Pensions funds
Pension funds can invest up to 49 per cent of a total portfolio in foreign equities, with no more than 10 per cent in any one equity. No single investment may be more than ten per cent of the total capital of the listed company.

Insurance companies
Insurance companies can invest 20 per cent of total funds in foreign equities, with no more than five per cent in one company. Investment in OTC stocks is not allowed.

Investment trusts
No overall limits, but no single investment may exceed five per cent of the total portfolio; and no holding may represent more than ten per cent of the capital of the listed company. Investment in OTC stocks is not allowed.

Switzerland

Pensions funds
Up to ten per cent of total funds may be invested in foreign equities, provided that no more than five per cent is invested in a single equity (including convertibles). Investment must be in listed companies on major exchanges.

Insurance companies
Up to 10 per cent of premium reserve stock may be allocated to foreign equities, with a five per cent limit on any single equity. Investment must be made through the major international exchanges.

In the Netherlands and Belgium, there are no limitations on institutions as to the extent of their foreign equity portfolios. Similarly there are no limitations in Italy, except that investment may only be in listed companies on major exchanges.

In Ireland, all investment institutions are restricted to 12.5 per cent of total funds under management for foreign equity investment. There is also a restriction on individuals, who may only invest up to $8,000 in foreign equities.

There are no restrictions in the UK or Spain.

Advantage Britain – but not for long

British companies have had much longer experience of international interest in their securities than most other European firms (although majors in Sweden, the Netherlands and Switzerland particularly have also enjoyed – or suffered – similar attention). The British have seen (or should have – many didn't notice) the effects of exchange controls being lifted, leaving them competing with foreign firms for UK-managed capital. They should, therefore, be better prepared for more open competition for funds.

Yet there are signs that many continental companies have been quicker to recognize the potential benefits and dangers. The determination of the Paris and Amsterdam Bourses, and others, not to be relegated to London – satellite status has a lot to do with this. It was no coincidence that 1988 saw the agreements on harmonizing EEC financial regulations hardening, and also the formation of a French IR society, CLIFF (Cercle de Liaison des Informations Financières en France). CLIFF's creation owes much to the foresight of the Bourse, which imposed a requirement that every listed company must have a nominated spokesman. Members of CLIFF visited both the USA and the UK within their first year and continue to tour capital markets to catch up with more experienced IR managers elsewhere.

European attitudes to neighbouring equity markets is illustrated by the fact that there are fewer of them listed in European exchanges (excluding their home markets) than there are US companies. Even the more internationally-conscious British have listed more companies in the USA than in any continental market.

While virtually every week sees two or more UK companies presenting to US fund managers, French and German brokers have expressed surprise if they see two in a month. Yet, language barriers aside, listings in Europe are much less complicated and expensive than those in Japan or the USA.

Whether or not there is any long-term value in share listings on more than one European exchange remains to be seen, although present restrictions prevent funds in some countries investing in shares which are not listed there. But there can be no question that IR programmes will have to be extended across Europe, even for those companies which have less-than-global ambitions. And it is clear that the window of opportunity is still open for the moment. Very few European companies have taken Europe seriously, and those that do will be a long step ahead.

Regulation – a changing scene

Again, the morass of regulations and customs defy the scope of this book – and the rate of change renders them a moveable target in any case. The aspiring – and persistent – IR manager can usually collect sufficient advice from competing banks and consultancies or he can consult companies who have preceded him. The Investor Relations Society can identify those of his opposite numbers that already bear the scars of this battlefield.

Switzerland – cosy cartel

However, some of the main differences can be illustrative. The requirements for listing on the Swiss Exchanges are similar – though less drastic – to those in Japan, and reflect the cosy cartel of three leading banks (Union Bank of Switzerland, Swiss Bank Corp and Credit Suisse) that seem to own the country! You will need 250 shareholder accounts valued at SwF ten million through these banks before you can list.

But Switzerland is still the biggest European investor in other European equity markets and will clearly be an important IR target for some time to come. Not only the big three banks, but also hundreds of smaller banks, manage huge amounts of money deposited in the famous Swiss numbered bank accounts, as well as in the more normal insurance, pension and other funds.

You would do well to keep the private accounts in mind, since they affect the attitudes of the fund managers, who really do have a preference for well-known companies or those with a simple story for them to put to those clients who have the temerity to ask them to justify their decisions.

One of the few continental specialist IR consultancies is based here – Hannan Associates – and can give useful advice, although its experience is primarily in looking after US companies, with their superficial knowledge of anything foreign.

EEC – co-operation or competition?

On the whole, the financial scene is changing so rapidly in the EEC that it might seem tempting to postpone consideration of listings until EEC harmonization plans become clearer. On the other hand, one must assume that a clearer picture will attract a rush of interest and hence more competition for investors' attention. It is certainly not difficult to get a step ahead at the moment, since so few companies have any organized IR programme underway. Whether or not listings are considered worthwhile at this point, there can be little doubt that an IR programme will win attention more easily now than it will when everyone else finally recognizes the potential.

The largest exchanges in the EEC are London, Frankfurt, Paris, Brussels and Amsterdam, with the second league including Milan, Munich and Madrid. The rate of change, though, is dramatic, with London, Paris, Madrid, Brussels and Copenhagan having deserted trading floors in favour of electronic systems.

Germany – bankers' domain

German companies – like those in Japan – have traditionally been funded, and largely owned, by banks and have only very recently shown signs of emerging into the world securities markets.

In Frankfurt, there are $200 billion in corporate pension funds alone – and up to 49 per cent can be invested abroad (and this figure includes bonds and investments). A German language prospectus will be required, with various concessions to local regulations – though nothing arduous. The major foreign securities houses have little influence unless a local bank is also involved, but these are running hard to catch up with the rest of the world.

France – still French!

Paris is next and the Commission de l'Opération des Bourses (better known as COB) is rapidly deregulating the market to avoid London monopolizing the future. It will – of course – insist on a French language prospectus and a translation of the chairman's annual statement, but it will also protect French newspapers from the ravages of Maxwell and Murdoch by forcing you to publish every company announcement as a paid advertisement. Their insurance companies can invest in foreign shares to *any* extent – *but only* if they're quoted in Paris! The other requirements are not difficult to meet and non-French houses are rapidly buying up French brokers. In the meantime, Paribas, BNP and Credit Lyonnais are among the key banks.

Netherlands – cheap and cheerful

Amsterdam is probably the most easily available European exchange, besides London, and has well-established procedures for foreign listings – mostly set up originally for Americans, who mistakenly thought this would become the major continental bourse. English language is more acceptable than elsewhere – even for the prospectus. Fees are low, the authorities are helpful, but bear in mind that Holland is a small market. AMRO and ABN are clear leaders in banking / broking.

Belgium – international but bi-lingual!

Brussels, too, is well-used to American listings – the EEC Commission's home looked like a good place for a European head office, and certainly allowed investor and government relations to share facilities. Furthermore, the local market is so small that the Belgian funds have had no choice but to invest abroad: the pension funds are estimated to have 56 per cent of their funds invested internationally, with about half of it in equities. Listing requirements are fairly liberal but the twin language problem can be a complicating factor – not least in the choice of sponsoring banks, with Société Générale and Banque Bruxelles de Lambert based in the French-speaking area and Kredietbank in the Flemish-speaking zone. Like Switzerland, Belgium has a well-established investor relations consultancy – James Kuhn Associates – which specializes in helping foreign, particularly US, companies.

Italy – still for the Romans

Italy should be a major market, but tends to be a lower priority for most outsiders. Settlement of equity trades has caused several scandals – though, as yet, nothing to match its banking scandals. Probably only worth considering if you have major operations there.

Spain – not yet!

Other European – and Scandinavian – countries are generally a considerably lower priority except for those companies with major operations in them. Of them all, perhaps Madrid merits a mention, since Spain is attracting so many foreign-owned operations.

The Madrid exchange will currently list only those companies which are at least partly-owned by Spaniards – hence the listings of majority-owned subsidiaries of Renault and Nissan. However, Madrid is currently preparing for deregulation (a series of pops rather than one big bang) and is expected to accept listings from wholly-foreign firms within a year or two. Regulations are not yet settled but there are several big local brokers and banks establishing relationships at present, and keeping interested parties informed.

Other markets

Of the remaining markets, Sweden and Luxemburg are probably the most internationally-minded and Lisbon, Athens and Oslo the least. But none of them will be important to any but a handful of companies.

Divided loyalties

Good advice is hard to find, except country by country. Credit Suisse First Boston probably has more pan-European experience and capability than any other bank. The second league would probably include Shearson Lehman and Merrill Lynch from the USA, Paribas, and several of the major UK houses, although many others – such as Morgan Stanley, Daiwa, AMRO and Deutsche – are trying hard to catch up.

Several of the large financial PR outfits claim to have some pan-European capability but they, too, are changing almost daily and the only safe course is to ask for a list of offices and their managers (are they local?) and a client list (ring a few, of *your* choice, for testimonials).

Dutch – or double-Dutch?

The difficulty, of course, is that this is still a much-divided market. Many European companies are only required to report results once a year, and are measured by very different criteria. This makes it difficult to present your performance in terms familiar to each market. Yet, European investors are becoming more international and, with a little care, you can now attract an audience of international specialists in most key cities. They will understand most of the widely-accepted accounting criteria and will usually decline simultaneous translation equipment (though this should not lull you into a false sense of security – most of them will certainly absorb less than the 20 per cent we are told to expect).

In Belgium, even some of the locals do their presentations in English to avoid the dual language (Flemish and French) dilemma. In the Netherlands, your employees are likely to split between Dutch and Turkish. The Germans are likely to be insulted if you assume they do not understand English and some of the French will still take offence if you assume they do.

The best compromise is probably to have your host banker or one of your local managers introduce you properly, and then for the chairman/CEO to show willing by saying good afternoon, and then flattering them by pointing out that their English is likely to be better than his French (or whatever). Be sure to give your banker or local manager a first draft for the introduction, though – many of them will know shamefully little about the company and may well make a very embarrassing mess of it.

Also, make sure you understand local attitudes – at least the crucial ones. The Swiss are likely to ask you more about your country's politics and the future of its currency than about your company. The French will be deeply impressed if you *have* run a successful French company with French managers for a considerable time, whilst the Germans may be more impressed if you have put your own German-speaking man in to run the show.

Most European fund managers are content to see the top team once a year, and a week will certainly cover five or six cities if you work on it. Lower-level, less formal meetings in between times also go down well with many, though, and your sponsoring bank should certainly be kept in regular touch.

Who owns the stock?

As with other foreign areas, tracking shareholdings can be a nightmare in Continental Europe. In several countries – most notably France and Switzerland – you will have no record whatsoever of your shareholders; the sponsoring banks will sell bearer certificates and you advertise the availability of reports, etc, through the Press. You will be required to deliver a certain number of them (or, at least, of the translated chairman's statement and summary figures) to the bank and you will never see proof of whether they have been distributed or not.

Many European funds are required to publish details of their major holdings – but only once a year and it is a big job to check them all. Some will even be embarrassed if you let them know that you know! As we've said, this is not really an important problem in defensive terms – you could take powers to disenfranchise them and the determined predator can build up a stake without you knowing early enough, whether or not you are listed abroad. But from the IR viewpoint it is highly frustrating not to be able to track ownership changes to refine your programme.

EEC discussions include some draft proposals – as do some more global debates – to improve ownership transparency. In the meantime, some consultancies can give limited help and there is nothing like keeping in touch with the markets to maintain a 'feel' for what is happening.

One market?

Europe is decidedly not yet a single market.

However, it shows every sign of developing at least into a federal system which has some common features. The accelerating trend towards harmonization and regional, industrial consolidation leaves companies little choice but to take Europe more seriously.

Some companies – and countries – will do so more willingly, quickly and effectively than others. Some – Rowntree, for example – started galloping around Europe too late.

PART IV

IS IT ALL WORTH IT?

CHAPTER 11

How long is a piece of string?
– *measuring IR effectiveness*

'If the share price has simply tracked the index for the last six years, why on earth are we spending all this money on you and your IR programme?'

Sadly, many company chairmen – and directors – still believe that IR is all about helping the share price, and they will tend to judge its effectiveness by that one criterion. But we have seen that IR is just as often about reining back a share price which is reflecting unrealistically high expectations. So how do you judge whether it's all worth it? How much does it cost anyway – and what is it worth?

Consolidated Goldfields reportedly spent £50 million on defending themselves against Minorco in early 1989. How much could they have saved if they hadn't been generally seen as poor managers in the first place? How much could GEC and Siemens have saved of the millions of pounds they spent to bid for Plessey, had their strategy and plans been better understood and accepted already? And how much would Tony Berry have spent on IR if he could have foreseen the problems that a failed Blue Arrow rights issue, and disgruntled Manpower franchisees, would bring him?

Counting the cost

We have advocated a co-ordinated – if not integrated – approach between IR and other forms of communication by the company, and

LEGAL ADVISERS TO COMPANIES INVOLVED IN
UK PUBLIC TAKEOVERS JANUARY – JUNE 1989
Ranked by value of takeover

Legal advisers	Number of deals	Value £m
1 Freshfields	11	10,143
2 Linklaters & Paines	11	9,878
3 Herbert Smith	15	3,324
4 Norton Rose	10	2,256
5 Slaughter and May	15	2,240
6 Clifford Chance	18	2,102
7 Ashhurst Morris Crisp	9	920
8 Allen & Overy	8	577
9 Nabarro Nathanson	6	558
10 Macfarlanes	6	555

Table based on completed and failed public takeover bids and includes only those advisers involved in two or more transactions

Source: Acquisitions Monthly

this can complicate the task of isolating the cost of the IR programme itself.

The annual report is a major part of the IR budget, but that is a legal obligation in any case. The cheapest way of producing an annual report likely to satisfy even an uncommunicative public company will probably cost at least £1 per copy. Simplifying the language and adding a few clear summaries, graphs, etc, could be done for very little more, although the colourful, well-designed output of an enlightened IR team may cost £2 or more per copy and the most grandiose up to £5 each.

Excluding the annual report, most elements of an IR programme are relatively inexpensive, unless it includes regional shareholder meetings or overseas roadshows. Mr P W O'Brien of Manchester Business School studied IR for his MBA thesis and found that most large PLCs with IR programmes spend £250,000–500,000 on them (excluding annual reports). Those with regional meetings and the roadshows can easily spend several millions, but they usually aim to derive other benefits from them too – adding customers, employees, journalists, etc, to the invitation lists.

Certainly, a basic IR programme can be mounted very economically and it is likely that executive time will be the limitation, rather than budget.

Measuring success – or failure

Like other forms of marketing, IR is virtually impossible to measure using any one form of measurement. Share price – like product sales – can be influenced by many factors, both internal and external. Similarly, general attitudes towards the company will be affected more by its performance than by its IR – although a good IR programme should make that performance better known and understood.

But if shareholder credibility, and the board's commitment to the programme, are to be maintained, it is crucial that IR be measured as objectively as possible – and that the results be made known. All too often, an IR manager will satisfy himself that *he* is performing effectively but forget to make the board fully aware of it!

The key to this process is to measure progress against well-defined objectives – all of them. So if the programme is designed to maintain the share price through a series of share issues, increase employee and individual ownership, and attract more acquisition approaches, each of these elements will need measurement systems.

Since IR objectives can vary so widely, the methods of measurement will be highly varied too. However, there are elements which cover most of the more obvious IR objectives and which can be measured, such as:

- corporate profile
- share performance
- investor support
- changes in share ownership
- investor attitudes.

The key to all measurement systems is to devise relative measures so as to exclude, as far as possible, external factors. These may be of the 'before and after' or 'compared to others' variety, but should always be built in where possible, since simple measures so often fail to convince ('of course the share price is up 20 per cent but then Guildford Widgets is up by 40 per cent!').

Corporate profile – measuring the soft sell

One of the most common mistakes is to *set too much* store by 'corporate image'. Most chief executives enjoy seeing their pictures and yards of press coverage in the FT but fail to recognize the pitfalls of this measure. After all, Clive Sinclair, Terence Conran, George Davies, Richard Branson *et al* could all have awarded themselves (or their PROs) top marks on editorial coverage, but all of them have been IR disasters, since IR is all about *long-term effects* – anyone can achieve a supercharged share price for a few weeks or months.

This is not to say that corporate profile is unimportant. It may be vital for the achievement of some corporate strategies. It is questionable whether BTR's failure to acquire Pilkington or Hanson Trust's difficulty over Imperial were about fundamental, objective weaknesses or about a general 'feeling' that both companies were bullying asset-strippers rather than good industrial managers.

Image, of course, can be measured by research studies and will probably form some part of any attitude surveys undertaken. There are, however, other – more quantifiable – measures of corporate profile which should be taken if they are appropriate. If the company is acquisitive, it will need acquisition suggestions from many sources – preferably from potential targets or bankers that have an 'in' with them. It should be simple to keep count of the number of such approaches over time and to see if different IR tactics affect the rate. Similarly, during a series of disposals, the number of potential buyers might be affected by IR activities.

Naturally, directors sceptical about IR will usually be pleased if none of the people they meet demonstrate knowledge of one of your IR messages, but it may be worth recording specific instances of this, if they are clearly identifiable as emanating from the IR programme, and particularly if they are of any significant value (eg, a business deal done as a result of such an approach).

Newspaper coverage, of course, is important and can be measured, but you should also measure your competitors' coverage and, ideally, devise methods of scoring positive and negative comments for each as well as tracking your success in obtaining favourable coverage of specific IR messages (eg, number of articles in which your description changes from 'ABC, the rapacious conglomerate' to 'ABC, the widget and grommet manufacturer').

Analysts' reports, too, should be carefully tracked. We look at the detail of them later, but a simple count of the number of research notes issued and the number of buy recommendations, over time, *relative* to your competitors, might help.

Does share performance matter?

Although it should not be the sole indicator, and should never be looked at simplistically, share performance obviously is a good measure. But price should not be seen in isolation from the market and should never be allowed to become a short-term obsession – chief executives who look up at their Stock Exchange or Reuters screens during every pause in the conversation are betraying not only their own ignorance but also the kind of short-termism of which many of them accuse investors.

It has been estimated that share prices are affected roughly evenly by the economy, the sector and the company's fundamentals. This is too simplistic since many factors will change this balance constantly, but it serves as a reminder that your share price means very little on its own.

Watching its performance relative to market indices (FTSE 100, etc) might exclude most of the general economic factors but can still over-simplify judgments, rendering it largely irrelevant as an IR measure-ment (with their UK indices at all-time highs recently, retailers were all very low because of interest rate fears, so Burton's IR man could not be blamed for his share price being low overall, or even for it being low against the index).

A good IR manager, of course, may be able to influence sentiment about his whole sector – or even country – but is better judged by his effect on the company's share performance. So he needs to draw up a peer group of companies against whom his company competes for investors' attention – ie, not *necessarily* direct competitors but those which *investors* compare it to.

Keep track of your share price against the relevant indices and against a group of five or so 'peer' companies. Datastream will provide such graphs easily or the numbers can be entered into a PC each day and printed out in tabular or graph form on demand. If your directors are particularly suspicious of your activity or you feel they need to be more aware of the company's position, it is simple to devise a PC programme which will produce an index for your peer group too and you can print out and circulate a table or graph every day, week or month to show how your shares are performing against the peer group *and* market indices over one, three, six and 12-month periods.

Even relative share price, though, gives only half the story. Your price can move very erratically if trading volume is very low or variable. If you aim to maintain a good price *and* sufficient support for any funding you plan, high (and, preferably, relatively stable) trading volume is important. To understand fully the market for your shares, therefore, you should be monitoring volume as carefully as price.

Not all stock exchanges yet report volume on every listed share. The main US exchanges do, and London does on the more active stocks, with European exchanges mostly a little behind. And if you have overseas listings, the volume of each exchange should be recorded, where possible.

Ideally, though, you will plot your trading volume, and those of your peer group and of the total market on the same graph as the prices. Now you can plot announcements, analysts' reports and IR events on the PC (or mark them on the printed graphs). If your shares diverge significantly from the peers and market, in price, volume or both, you should seek an explanation if your events calendar does not explain it.

These graphs, over time, provide an excellent measurement system, even enabling you to judge the effect of different forms of announcement, different analysts' research, different kinds of presentation, meetings, etc (even different team members attending them!).

To gain an even fuller picture, you can plot your company's key ratios relative to your peer group and to the market. 'Consensus forecasts' on major companies are now available in many markets and are eagerly used by fund managers (see Chapter 5). Investors use a wide variety of ratios to compare companies, but they are generally looking for: earnings (past and potential), income (dividends), assets or – particularly recently – cashflow. Working out your key ratios in past and expected performance, therefore, and tracking how they change relative to your peer group, can be a frighteningly effective method of measuring the effectiveness of the IR programme, since this largely removes company performance from the equation. We suggest a constant tracking of the price/earnings, price/dividend, price-to-book (assets) and price-to-cashflow ratios (see Glossary).

Particularly by tracking these graphs through periods of crisis or elation, you can learn important lessons for the future. If Guildford Widgets maintained a steadier price, volume and PE ratio than you in the weeks following the crash of October 1987, maybe they were doing a better job of discussing their recession plans with analysts – it would be worth asking some of the analysts that cover both of you (or looking at their reports on both of you, if you have them) to find out what was behind the difference.

Investor support – too little, too late?

Gaining, and maintaining, the support of investors for management's strategy and tactics is one of the fundamental objectives of every IR programme, and will sometimes provide the ultimate measure – your promotion or P45 when the bid succeeds or fails. Obviously, IR suddenly becomes a shared – and vital – responsibility of senior executives during a bid, and the results are all too obvious.

But it is all too easy to forget that there are ample opportunities for totally objective measurements of IR at other times through shareholder proxies. The company secretary will receive proxy cards and letters every year ahead of the AGM, as well as ahead of EGMs, during bids, etc. He will probably have a record of each vote for years past and these can give useful pointers to your effectiveness. While some of the issues are, in themselves, minor, the IR manager should concern himself with any issue on which shareholders are actually asked to vote, should ensure that the issues are adequately explained, and monitor the number of votes cast each way. Over time, the number of votes cast against *any* management proposals should drop if the IR programme is effective.

Similarly, the number of protest letters should fall if you are explaining management decisions better. If you have an 0800 telephone line for shareholders, you could have every call logged (or recorded) with a note of any negative feedback.

Share ownership – voting with their feet

The most obvious, direct, quantifiable and final measure of IR, of course, is the share register. In the extreme, shareholders accepting a hostile bid for your company are voting with their feet. But there is constant change taking place in ownership and analysis of this will yield all sorts of information.

First, if private shareholders are important to you, it is child's play to keep count of the number of private investors buying and selling each month. Clearly, there will always be some individuals who sell your shares for reasons of personal circumstance, but there is nothing to stop you contacting a few every so often (directly or through a research survey) to find out *why* they've sold. The same applies to institutions – you will not know whether they have sold as part of a policy move from UK equity into US pork-belly futures or whether they have suddenly taken the view that you are about to go bankrupt, unless you ask them.

Certainly, a running measure of how many holders sell out altogether each month can – over time – be one useful measure of overall IR effectiveness.

But a surfeit of sellers over buyers will often have shown up in the share performance long before the names hit the register and go through the 212 analysis (see Chapter 3). Analysis of the share register should, though, provide much more useful measurement of IR effectiveness if you go back to the objectives.

Only the most unusually lucky (or ignorant and short-sighted) company will be totally satisfied with the composition of its shareholder base when it first embarks on a proper IR programme. Therefore, changes in ownership are almost certain to be amongst your objectives – whether you are a British Telecom, dissatisfied with the cost of having too many very small holders; a BP concerned that it has too few private holders; or a Glaxo with a majority of its sales overseas and a wish to match that with ownership.

If a different ownership pattern is among the objectives, your effectiveness should be relatively easy to demonstrate. The share register should easily yield a direct measure of the proportions of private, institutional and foreign ownership. At a deeper level, you should have chosen particular types of institution (those with investment criteria which suit your expected performance – see Chapter 3) and targeted specific funds, so you can measure your success by monitoring their shareholdings individually and collectively. For example, if you were surprised to learn that 26 of the top 50 pension funds were light or non-holders, analyze them again each year for an overall measure and monitor the Coal Board and Postal Funds, which were specific targets, once a year. Prepare a report on your successes (and failures) against each ownership objective – these will be the most objective statistics you can obtain.

Investor attitudes – essential feedback

Share performance and investor support are the most direct forms of feedback, but many investors will not sell their shares or vote against the board even when they are quite seriously dissatisfied with the company or something it is doing. Frequently, small concerns will build up which are based on misunderstandings that could easily be corrected if they were known. In the final analysis, inertia might prevent the hostility being expressed until the predator's offer arrives.

It is therefore important to monitor investors' concerns through some form of attitude research, and this also provides an extremely valuable measurement of IR progress and methods.

Various independent research firms offer a wide range of alternative methods which are effective and fairly cheap. The main types of research used are: individual surveys commissioned by companies directly; omnibus surveys, which cover large numbers of companies but where you can pay to add a few questions and receive the results; and co-operative surveys which are between the two and cover several companies. Separate surveys are necessary if you wish to cover both institutional and private investors, but both can build up into a useful picture of shareholders' knowledge about, and attitudes to, the company and how these are changing in response to the IR programme. Costs for these professional surveys will vary according to the route you choose, the sample size and the method and length of questioning. However, as a rough guide, one full survey is likely to cost about £12–15,000.

Single-company surveys

BPRI, which undertook some of our research for this book, is one of several agencies which offers to do individual company surveys, and points out that the main advantages of this route are that you have complete control of the questions (subject to their professional advice and ethics, of course) and timing. Most surveys of institutional investors cover:

- awareness of the company relative to its peers
- knowledge of the company's activities and performance
- attitudes to the company, relative to its peers, in terms of value, prospects, management quality, etc
- main concerns and attractions of the company
- assessment of the company's communications.

Financial journalists and analysts are often covered together with fund managers, and interviews are usually by telephone questionnaire – although longer, face-to-face 'qualitative' interviews are sometimes added.

By making sure that at least one question in the first part of the 'knowledge' part of the questionnaire relates to a specific and recent IR message, you will be able to test your communication channels as well as checking whether or not investors' knowledge about the company is improving.

Asking if your shares, and those of your peer group, are under, fully, or over-valued will give a good idea of investors' relative valuations and how these change, while the questions on management quality, prospects, etc may not give an absolute measure (the sample is too small) but the trend over the years will give a fascinating insight.

So, too, will the main concerns and attractions, which should pick up those unspoken – and sometimes unexpected – worries in the market, and help you to improve your messages to meet investors' needs.

Finally, the communication part might test changes in the annual report and views of your IR programme relative to those of your peer group. It can also include a question for fund managers only about which analysts they rate highly for advice on your shares.

Private shareholders – forgotten majority

A survey of some of the private shareholders every year might also expose some unexpected concerns – is the registrar failing to keep their addresses up to date, do they wish you would introduce a scrip dividend issue, or would they prefer a short-form annual report? There may be bigger worries, too, like fears over your entry into waste disposal, new high-tech research or high-street loans.

These are all worth discovering while you still have time to explain your strategy, but private investor research can also be useful to discover the age and sex profile of your shareholders, whether they inherited or chose your shares (in the latter case, who advised them), which newspapers they read (in case you need to advertise to reach them in a crisis), what other shares they own and how often – if ever – they change their portfolio. If you have a shareholder meetings programme, you can ask what they liked and disliked about the meeting, in order to refine the format and style.

Omnibus surveys – superficial but wider

Several research firms offer standing surveys to which you can add your company and one or two questions. Essentially, they use a regular panel of investors and their advisers (parallel surveys cover journalists, senior businessmen, politicians, unions, etc) to answer a questionnaire once or twice each year.

Because these surveys cover a large number of companies, you will not be able to ask many specific questions or add many specific people to the list, but you will obtain a measure of your company relative to very many more companies than you could afford to cover in an individual survey. If you are starting up research for the first time, it may even be worth buying into an omnibus survey before commissioning your own – it could form a useful baseline for further questions.

The best-known UK omnibus studies are those conducted by Market and Opinion Research International (MORI), run by Bob Worcester, whose 'familiarity/favourability' theories are well-known and well-proven and who has many years' experience in this field.

Interviews with fund managers are face-to-face and last for about an hour. Analyst interviews are much shorter, since they only cover one or two sectors, and are by telephone. The numbers interviewed by MORI have grown over the years – in the autumn survey of 1988, 147 institutions were questioned (all with at least £10m under management) and 385 analysts. The analysts are selected in consultation with the client companies who name the analysts they are in touch with or want included in the survey for other reasons.

The analysts in a given sector will then be asked about that sector generally, as well as about its constituent companies. But, arguably, a problem with multi-client studies is that respondents' comments on some sectors will be much better informed than on others, and it is difficult to assess the impact of this variation on the final results. Also, the timing cannot be varied to suit you and, if the survey closely followed your results or some other major announcement, you could obtain a seriously distorted view of investor attitudes.

Co-operative research – a useful compromise?

Between the single client and multi-client research formats is the co-operative survey, such as the Investor Relations Guide, launched in 1988 by City Research Associates. This programme breaks down into three modules: the professionals programme; the private shareholder programme; and a combined programme covering both professional investors and individual shareholders. Clients can select the elements that they want.

The professionals programme divides into two stages: the first is a report of a general survey, conducted by telephone among 500 institutional investors, stockbrokers and financial and business journalists. It covers the factors influencing investment decisions, sources of information, views about the general prospects for the different major Stock Market sectors and key IR priorities.

The second stage is the sector report which is a multi-client study, but for client companies all within the same sector. Clients subscribing to the programme can have some input into the structuring of the questionnaire and some influence on who should be included in the list of 100 interviewees. For this survey, interviews are face-to-face, not by telephone, and take about an hour.

Subscribing clients can also opt to have included in the questionnaire a limited number of questions on their own (exclusive) behalf. The answers to these remain confidential to the client concerned. An advantage of this 'in-between' approach would seem to be that all the interviewees will be knowledgeable about their sector – and the variation in their level of knowledge about the different companies being covered is not likely to be very great.

Other opinion formers

When measuring the effectiveness of the IR programme, it's worth remembering the influence which investor relations activity has on audience groups outside the investment community – customers, suppliers, employees, parliamentarians and government departments.

All of these groups are likely to follow comments on the company which are made by the financial press; many may see brokers' circulars on the company; the company may have to present itself to the Office of Fair Trading or the Monopolies and Mergers Commission and may find questions being asked about it in the Houses of Parliament; trade union representatives will follow the fortunes of the company as a precursor to the next round of wage negotiations. Investor relations messages need to be consistent with other corporate messages and the attitudes of all the company's external and internal audiences need to be tested on a regular basis.

This can be done separately from the investor surveys, or in parallel with them. Certainly, financial journalists and stockbrokers' analysts can be included and civil servants, customers and suppliers, employees and union leaders can be interviewed by the same research firms, but usually in separate surveys.

Omnibus surveys of these audiences can be added to the research programme. Again, MORI has studies covering most of them and there are various other well-established panels in every area.

Presenting the findings to management

As everyone knows, there is nothing more absorbing than hearing new information about oneself – especially when it concerns how others rate your performance at a particular activity. This is no less true of a company's senior management digesting research findings which disclose how the owners of the company rate their ability to manage it – particularly when they also know that existing and potential investors rate 'quality of management' as the most important aspect of the company when investment decisions are being made.

When Jack Benny said, on receiving an acting award, 'I don't deserve this, but then, I have arthritis and I don't deserve that either,' he expressed the reaction that company directors often have when exposed to research findings. It is probably sensible to ask a representative of the research firm to present the research findings and to draw the appropriate conclusions – so increasing the likelihood of the messenger being shot rather than the instigator of the research!

At the same time, it is important to point out that investor comments relayed back to the directors are, of course, subjective and reflect the view of one individual and not necessarily the investment community as a whole. Some of the findings may be fairly depressing and you'll have a worse IR problem if the CEO takes them so much to heart that he jumps from his top-floor window!

Nonetheless, it can be a useful exercise, over the years, to count the number of positive comments made, as well as bad ones, and see how they shift in one direction or the other. All the research findings will be indicative rather than absolute, and it is therefore important to keep the findings in perspective.

For the same reason, outside research on investors' attitudes probably should not be presented in isolation. Ideally, the IR manager will set them in context by presenting his analysis of the company's relative share performance, and of the changes achieved in the share register, together with his reports on the other measures we have discussed. If he has analyzed the effect of each IR event to the extent of comparing the success (or failure) of each director involved, he should keep his conclusions to himself!

CHAPTER 12

To be, or not to be, a global stock?
– *some final thoughts*

'**Our goal is to tell you the business facts that we would want to know if our roles were reversed.**' (Our friend Warren E Buffet in his 1988 chairman's statement.)

We have tried to review the benefits, pitfalls and current state of play of investor relations from the point of view of the relatively uninitiated. Much more could be said – and probably will be – but our aim was to lay down some foundations, not to try to have the last word.

British companies, in particular, allowed union shop stewards largely to gain control of their employee communications over many years, and the 1980s have been a more painful period of readjustment than might otherwise have been necessary because of the 'them and us' attitudes which this encouraged, and because of the lack of communication skills and channels which resulted.

Similarly, many British companies have grown used to relying on a small group of stockbrokers' analysts to keep their owners informed. Some of them have already had vivid demonstrations of the support this has won them – very few have retained their independence once a serious bid was launched – and this in a decade when investors have enjoyed unusually good returns on their shares.

Signs of acceleration in hostile bid activity have emerged in even those bastions of financial prudence, Germany and Japan. Some argue that it is no longer poor companies who are the targets – increasing sophistication amongst *financial* bidders now means that even highly-respected companies are falling prey if they allow their share prices to fall below their real value.

Cross-border equity investment, according to Salomon Brothers, now totals about $640 billion, over six per cent of the total world market's capitalization. UK investors are still the largest players, with two per cent of all foreign equity investment, but Japanese, American and Continental European investors are catching up quickly. About 20 per cent of all UK equity trading is done by foreigners already and this total is growing. Many European stocks are being traded more actively on foreign exchanges than in their home markets and cross-border trading in 1989 is expected to breach 1987's records easily. We would regard some form of Pan-European exchange – formal or informal – as inevitable, and very important.

Most European companies are – perhaps belatedly – beginning to recognize the need for a more active investor relations approach and experienced IR executives are increasingly being asked to give advice to chairmen and other directors who are trying to establish programmes. If they do so before they face a hostile bid, a business or financial crisis or a market/industry collapse, and if they can define clear strategies and objectives, there is no reason why it should prove to be too daunting a task.

IR is, though, no panacea for business ills. A good IR programme will not very often save a poor company – though it may gain it time to transform itself. Nor is IR a crutch which can be cast aside when the injury is healed. To be successful, it must be a way of life – it must include a long-term commitment to the rights of investors to have adequate information, to enable them to assess the company's current and long-term value. It is a time consuming, often frustrating and sometimes expensive discipline. It will require substantial support from the chairman, chief executive, financial director and other board members. It will require a senior executive to plan and execute the programme, and co-operation from many members of the functional and line staffs. Defining the corporate strategy in absolutely clear terms, and setting appropriate IR objectives, will concentrate management minds – if not change them – while researching existing and suitable potential investors will try patiences. And, after all this, the attempt to win support for the management's policies may even call into question their viability.

Success, though, can bring rich rewards. Surviving the many perils which may arise could make it all worthwhile. But so could a higher valuation, the avoidance of expensive and humiliating failures to win support for a new move and the achievement of improved commercial reputation and employee morale and loyalty.

The good company will be responsive to its customer needs in everything it does. We would argue that investors are the customer for much of the company's productive effort. If they are not offered a suitable product, they will not offer much for it. Even if they *are* offered a suitable product, they will only pay the top price if they believe the person who is selling it to them. So IR is not about shouting indiscriminate messages to ill-chosen crowds. It is about *consistently* delivering the right messages, to the right people – and listening to their doubts, needs and reactions. It is immediately tied into corporate strategy.

As in all other fields of business, the starting point must be to secure the home market first – and then expand sensibly. We have argued that much can be achieved without expensive and time-consuming foreign travel, because much of the foreign investment is done through a company's home market. And even if foreign exposure is judged worthwhile, the IR profile and priorities should be carefully planned for each area – only fee-earning banks will argue that listings and share issues are necessary every time. But if penetration of Japan is planned in five years' time, the company can wait five years and then launch an expensive programme, or it can start a measured build-up now. The Japanese car and consumer electronics companies have amply demonstrated the value of long-term planning of market penetration; Rowntree, Distillers and others have demonstrated the dangers of marketing complacency.

Do you expect your company to need the support of domestic or international investors – for offensive or defensive purposes – in the next ten years? If so, where – and what plans have you made? If the answer is none, good luck!

Investor relations summarized

Its purpose

To attain, and retain, the highest share price that is consistent with an accurate and informed view of the company's relative performance and potential.

Whose responsibility?

Ultimately, the *chief executive's*. He must be closely involved in developing the objectives and strategy for the IR programme which reflect and support the company's long-term business goals.

Other members of the IR team must include:

- The *finance director*, so that financial data can be collated, strategic messages built-up for transmission to the investment community and an intelligent reception given to any messages that come back.

- The *company secretary*, whose role it is to ensure that the share register is kept up to date and designed to provide information about shareholder demographics at great speed when needed to keep those on the IR team informed of any significant changes on the register and to ensure that the IR process complies with all the regulations that apply.
- The *IR manager*, whose job it is to design corporate messages which accurately reflect the overall business objectives of the company and to drive and co-ordinate the IR programme.

Qualities needed by the IR manager

Appointment must be made at a senior level so that the IR manager is close enough to the people running the company (or be one of them) to be able to interpret facts and events properly on the company's behalf. Financial, company and sector knowledge are essential pre-requisites but, most importantly, he must be a communicator with marketing skills.

Defining the audience

The company's own current and likely performance will, to a large extent, dictate the kinds of investor who will be best suited to, and attracted to, the shares of the company.

Analyse the share register and see where the imbalances lie. Audiences will comprise:

Investors

- institutional investors (pension fund managers, insurance companies, unit trust groups and investment trusts)
- government (as an investor)
- charities (eg, the church commissioners)
- banks
- brokers (as fund managers)
- other companies
- overseas investors
- individual investors
- employees as investors.

Advisers

- brokers
  - analysts

- sales teams
- financial media

Executing the programme

Design messages which reflect and support the company's objectives and likely performance; and communication programmes which reach defined audiences in a timely and effective manner. The main channels of communication are:

- annual report and accounts
- interim report
- company fact books
- databases and directories
- advertising
- company announcements
- meetings and presentations
- AGMs and shareholder meetings

IR in special situations

Tracking issues

'An issue ignored is a crisis ensured'. Track legislature in countries where the company has operations to be prepared to lobby against new laws being considered, or make provision to accept them and sometimes turn them to competitive advantage.

Dealing with takeovers

- Have in place contingency plans to fend off unwelcome takeovers; rehearse them from time to time.
- Decide in advance, the members of the takeover or defence team and ensure they can be relieved of their day-to-day duties to concentrate on implementing the bid or defence strategy.
- Be clear about the defence strategy *before* the bid materializes.

Credit ratings

- IR function must embrace relationships with the credit-rating agencies as debt financing grows in importance.
- Keep the agencies briefed, in advance, of every significant move the company is about to make (erring on the side of caution) to prevent a ratings slide.

New share issues

Anticipate possible concerns by existing shareholders and prepare literature and presentations which pursuade them that the investment is right for the company.

International IR

Reasons for:

- Increased funding options through global and regional (eg, EEC) security markets.
- Increased valuation in home and overseas markets.
- Support for acquisition programmes.
- Support for existing business operations.
- Enlargement of employee share ownership.
- Plan the programme well in advance.

Action:

- Select and check out competent advisors.
- Prioritize markets; if possible, 'break the ground' by running overseas roadshows before seeking a listing.
- Meet with foreign fund managers in London to provide a firm base for overseas activities and management exposure to the different styles of foreign investors.
- Be clear about the objectives for overseas activity and ensure that management is committed, in the long term, to putting up with the rigours of constant overseas travel.

Measuring the effectiveness of the programme

- Measure progress against well-defined objectives, eg, maintaining the share price through a series of share issues or attracting more acquisition approaches.
- Through research, measure progress against 'common' IR objectives such as:
  corporate profile
  share performance
  investor support
  changes in share ownership
  investor attitudes
- Ensure that the company's performance is measured against that of its peer group.

GLOSSARY

Many of the definitions in this glossary inevitably refer to other words or phrases which may not always be understood. If you come across such a word or phrase, the first thing to do is look for its alphabetical position in the glossary; failing that, in the index.

Accepting House: A financial institution, usually a merchant bank, which for a fee will guarantee the payment of a bill of exchange.

Acid Test Ratio: Yardstick of a firm's ability to pay its debts due in the near future. Ratio of liquid assets (cash + debtors) divided by current liabilities. Usually close to 1.0.

Advance Corporation Tax (ACT): Part of corporation tax liability, payable (at basic rate of income tax on *gross* dividends) at same time as net dividends, set off later against 'mainstream' tax.

American Depository Receipt (ADR): Certificate issued by depository bank showing number of American depository shares held by owner.

Annualized Cost: Annuity which, over a known number of years and at a known discount rate, is equivalent to the present value of a particular cash amount.

Annuity: Regular annual amount for a given number of years (in personal affairs, until death).

Arbitrage: Buying in one market and selling in another to gain from price differences (which this process will reduce but, due to transaction costs, not eliminate).

Asset: Valuable resource owned by a business, acquired at a measurable money cost. Examples: factory, equipment, stocks of materials.

Asset Turnover: Annual sales revenue divided by net assets.

Bad Debt: Debt reckoned to be uncollectable.

Balance Sheet: Statement showing assets and liabilities of a business at a given date.

Bank of England: UK central bank whose main responsibility is integrity of the currency. Also represents official 'authorities' in controlling City institutions and markets.

Bank Overdraft: Facility for borrowing from bank on current account up to agreed limit. Amount borrowed, and interest rate, may fluctuate.

Bankruptcy: Legal process occurring when individual cannot pay liabilities. For companies, called 'liquidation' (or 'winding-up').

Barter: Process of exchanging goods against other goods rather than money.

Bear: Speculator who expects prices to fall, who may sell assets he does not own, hoping to buy back later at a profit.

Beta: Coefficient relating the sensitivity of an investment's return to that of the whole market (according to MPT).

Bill of Exchange: Post-dated cheque which the recipient can 'discount', to receive cash now in return for an interest payment.

Bond Borrowings: Represented by certificates issued by the company, which can be traded between lenders.

Bonus Issue: = 'scrip issue'. Issue of additional shares pro rata to existing shareholders in return for no cash or other assets. Usually used to split shares to obtain lower unit prices.

Book Value: Balance sheet amount shown for asset, normally original (HC) cost less any amounts written off.

Break-up Value: Estimated amount realisable for asset on 'break-up' or scrapping, net of disposal costs.

Building Society: Financial institution which receives personal savings and provides loan mortgage funds for people wanting to buy houses, at a variable interest rate.

Bull: Speculator who expects prices to rise, who may buy assets (or options to acquire them) hoping to sell them later at a profit.

Business Risk: The volatility of a business's operating profits (or cash flows), due to the particular assets in which funds are invested, regardless of how those assets are financed.

Capital Allowance: Tax equivalent of depreciation of fixed assets, calculated according to Inland Revenue rules.

Capital Budgeting: Planning use of investment funds, usually including methods of evaluating capital investment projects.

Capital Employed: = Net Assets. Shareholders' funds + long-term debt.

Capital Gain: Part of 'return' on investment in securities, stemming from increase in market value, not from dividends or interest.

Capital Market Line (CML): Straight line, originating at 'risk-free rate of return, showing relationship of return to market risk.

Capital Rationing: Artificial, often temporary, limitation of amount of funds available for investment, often self-imposed.

Capitalising Factor: Coefficient to translate expected future income into a present 'capital' value, e.g. price/earnings ratio.

Cash: Legal tender banknotes and coins. In accounting usually includes amounts 'owed' to firms by banks on current or deposit account.

Cash Discount: Reduction in price of goods sold, offered in return for prompt settlement by debtor.

Cash Flow: Usually defined as 'retained profits plus depreciation' for a period = 'Internally-generated cash flow'.

Central Bank: Banker to government and to commercial banks, often with a monopoly over issue of banknotes. In UK, the Bank of England.

Certificate of Deposit (CD): Interest-bearing acknowledgement of deposit with a financial institution, usually repayable within months.

Clearing Bank: Major bank (e.g. Barclays, Lloyds, Midland, National Westminster) which exchanges cheques received from other clearing banks at a clearing house daily, settling only the net balance.

Collateral: Asset serving as security for loan.

Commercial Paper: Borrowings represented by certificates auctioned by the company's agent which he will buy back at face value.

Conglomerate: Diversified group of companies whose subsidiaries operate in unrelated areas.

Consolidated Accounts: Accounts for a group of companies, 'consolidated' by combining the separate assets and liabilities of all subsidiaries with those of the 'holding' company.

Constant Purchasing Power (CPP) Accounting: Method of inflation accounting which treats money amounts of various dates as 'foreign currencies', using the RPI as the 'exchange rate'.

Convertible Loan: Loan convertible, at holder's option, into ordinary shares on prearranged terms.

Corporation Tax: Tax payable by companies on taxable profits, either at 52 per cent or at reduced 40 per cent rate for smaller companies.

Cost of Capital: The criterion rate of return for capital investment projects, calculated as (risk-adjusted) weighted average of the marginal (after-tax) costs of ordinary, preference and debt capital.

Coupon Rate: Nominal rate of interest payable on fixed-interest securities.

Covenants: Conditions attached to loan agreement restricting borrower's freedom of action (eg, re dividends, working capital, etc).

Creditor: Person or company to whom money is due.

Criterion Rate: Required rate of return on capital investment project.

Cumulative: (of preference dividends). Any unpaid preference dividends must be made good before any ordinary dividend may be paid.

Currency Debasement: Process of reducing purchasing power of currency, originally by fraudulently adding base metal to precious metal, now by more sophisticated methods.

Current Asset: Cash or any asset expected to be converted into cash or consumed in normal course of business within 12 months from the balance sheet date. Examples: stocks, debtors.

Current Cost Accounting (CCA): System of current value (not 'inflation') accounting, which a government committee proposed instead of CPP.

Current Liability: Liability due to be paid within 12 months of balance sheet date. Examples: trade creditors, bank overdraft.

Current Ratio: Current assets divided by current liabilities. Measure of liquidity, usually expected to be between 1.5 and 2.0.

Debentures: Long-term liability (from the Latin: 'they are owed').

Debt (as opposed to Equity): Long-term liabilities.

Debt Ratio: Balance sheet measure of gearing. Long-term liabilities divided by total long-term capital employed (= debt plus equity).

Debtor: Person or firm which owes money to a business, usually in respect of goods or services supplied.

Deduction at Source: Process by which payer of wages or dividends deducts income tax (PAYE – Pay As You Earn – and ACT respectively) from amount paid to recipient and transmits it to Inland Revenue on his behalf.

Demand Deposit: Current Account deposit with bank which bears no interest and is withdrawable 'on demand' (ie, with no notice).

Depreciation: Amount written off cost of fixed asset in accounting period and charged as expense; spreads the total cost over the asset's whole life (usually in equal instalments).

Dilution: Process by which a shareholder's equity interest is reduced by a company issuing additional shares to other shareholders.

Discount Factor: Coefficient reducing future cash amounts to 'present value'.

Discount House: Financial institution which buys bills of exchange at 'discount' (below face value) and collects in full on maturity.

Discount Rate: Interest rate used in making present value calculations.

Discounted Cash Flow (DCF): Technique (eg, NPV, IRR) for evaluation capital projects, using interest rate as 'exchange rate over time'.

DCF Yield: DCF technique, also known as internal rate of return.

Disinvestment: Reducing investment by selling or abandoning asset(s).

Diversification: Adding or substituting investments with low or negative co-variance with existing holdings, to reduce total risk of portfolio.

Dividend: Cash paid to shareholder out of profits, if declared by a company's directors.

Dividend Controls: Statutory restrictions on amount of dividends payable by companies, in force in UK for 10 years between 1966 and 1979.

Dividend Cover: Earnings (either HC or CCA) divided by net dividends.

Dividend Payout Ratio (DPR): Reciprocal of dividend cover. Dividends payable as a percentage of profits available for a period.

Dividend Yield: Dividends per share for a year divided by market price. Usually *gross*; but *net* in equity share valuation formula.

Earnings Before Interest and Tax (EBIT): Operating profit for a year, used to calculate interest cover and return on net assets, ignoring complications of tax and gearing.

Earnings Per Share (EPS): Profit after tax and minority interests (see *profit attributable to ordinary shareholders*) divided by number of ordinary shares in issue.

Earnings Yield: EPS divided by market price per share.

EBIT Chart: Graph plotting EPS (on vertical axis) against EBIT level (on horizontal axis); used in making debt versus equity choice.

Equity: Residual financial interest in firm's assets. Usually means 'owners' equity', referring only to interests of ordinary shareholders (ie, excluding preference shareholders). Used by investors to mean total shareholders funds (share capital and resources).

Expected Value: Weighted average of subjective probabilities applied to all possible outcomes anticipated.

External Finance: Funds raised from 'outside' the company; such as issuing new equity shares for cash, borrowing.

Factor: Company which buys trade debts at a discount for cash.

Final Dividend: Second dividend for a year, after interim dividend.

Finance House: Company providing funds to finance HP and leasing.

Financial Lease: Lease giving lessee use of asset over most of its life, providing another way to finance its 'acquisition', in effect.

Financial Objective: (of a company). 'To maximize the wealth of the present ordinary shareholders.'

Financial Risk: Extra volatility of stream of equity earnings due to financial gearing, added to business risk (operational gearing).

Financial Goods: Stocks of completed manufactured products, held for sale.

First-year Tax Allowance: 100 per cent deduction from taxable profit allowed for tax purposes in respect of most purchases of capital assets.

Fixed Assets: Resource, either tangible or intangible, with relatively long life, acquired for use in producing goods or services, not for re-sale in the ordinary course of business.

Fixed Expenses: Expenses which (in the short term) do not vary with output. Examples: factory rent, administrative salaries.

Flat Yield: Interest yield ignoring capital gain (or loss) on maturity, calculable by dividing annual interest by current market price.

Floating Charge: Charge to creditor which is secured, not against specific assets, but which 'floats' over all (otherwise unsecured) assets, 'crystallizing' on occurrence of certain specified events.

Flowback: The repurchase in a company's home market or shares previously owned by foreign shareholders.

Forecasting: Guessing the uncertain future, often in quantified form.

Funds Flow Statement: Accounting statement showing sources and uses (or 'applications') of funds for a period.

Gearing: Proportion of debt in capital structure represents *financial* gearing; proportion of fixed expenses in total operating expenses represents operating (or 'business') gearing.

Gilt-edged Securities: UK government loan stocks.

Going Public: Issuing shares to the public for the first time.

Goodwill: Excess of purchase price paid on acquisition of another firm over net book value of tangible net assets.

Gross Dividend: Amount of dividend before deduction of basic rate income tax = Net dividends divided by $(100 -$ basic rate income tax) per cent.

Gross Fund: Institutional fund not subject to tax on dividends or capital gains. Example: pension fund.

Group Accounts: Consolidated accounts of all companies belonging to a group of companies with a common holding company.

Guarantee: Personal (or corporate) undertaking to be responsible for the debts of another (person or company) if nominal debtor is unable to pay in full. A personal guarantee by a majority shareholder in a limited company 'undoes' the limited nature of his liability.

Hire Purchase (HP): System of paying for an asset by instalments.

Holding Company: Company owning more than 50 per cent of equity shares in subsidiaries (directly or indirectly), or controlling composition of its board of directors = 'parent' company.

Horizon: Point of time in future beyond which financial calculations are not made explicitly (though including a 'terminal value' in capital project evaluation makes them *implicitly*).

Horizontal Merger: Combination of firms making the same product.

Income: American equivalent of profit. Hence operating income = operating profit, gross income = gross profit, and net income = net profit.

Income Tax: Tax payable on personal incomes (such as dividends or trading profits of sole traders or partnerships). Basic rate is 30 per cent, and graduated rates rise to a maximum 75 per cent on 'unearned' income.

Incremental Cash Flows: Cash flows which will occur as a result of action (eg, investing in capital project), but not otherwise.

Index-linking: Process of linking payment to the rate of inflation as measured by RPI. Examples: government securities, pensions, tax thresholds, capital gains (from April 1982).

Inflation: Rise in the 'general' level of money prices, measured by the (annual) increase in the Retail Price Index.

Inflation Accounting: Method of adjusting accounts using *money* as the unit of measurement on to a 'constant purchasing power' basis, by index-linking all amounts by references to the date incurred.

Inflation Premium: Part of the rate of interest, depending on the anticipated future rate of inflation.

Insolvency: Inability to meet financial obligations.

Institutions: Major organizations in the capital and money markets, such as insurance companies and pension funds.

Interest Cover: EBIT divided by annual interest payable.

Interest Rate: Annual rate of compensation for borrowing or lending (money) for a period of time, comprising: *(a) pure time-preference, (b) risk premium and (c) inflation premium.*

Interim Dividend: First (usually smaller) of two dividends paid in a year by company.

Intermediaries: Financial organizations which separate borrowing from lending and may alter the time-maturity of loans. They profit from economies of scale and specialization, and reduce the risk by diversification.

Internal Finance: Raising funds from 'within' a company, usually referring to retained profits plus depreciation (or perhaps selling off assets owned).

Internal Rate of Return (IRR): Rate of discount which, applied to a capital project, produces a zero NPV.

Introduction: Method of 'going public' without issuing any extra shares, by arranging for a Stock Exchange quotation for existing shares.

Investment (Real): Fixed capital formation; investment in fixed assets.

Investment (Financial): Acquisition of a security, often from existing holder on the secondary market. Hence 'financial' investment does *not* necessarily imply any 'real' investment.

Investment Trust: Company which holds a portfolio of (quoted) investments.

Irredeemable: Loan stock with no maturity date, whose annual interest is a 'perpetuity'.

Issuing House: Financial institution, usually a merchant bank, which arranges new issues of securities (and advises on terms).

Jobber: A person or firm on the Stock Exchange buying and selling shares (owned as principal) by quoting prices to stockbrokers (who act as agents for investors).

Jobber's Turn: Difference between buying price and selling price quoted.

Lease: Commitment (by the 'lessee') to pay rent to the owner ('lessor') in return for the use of an asset.

Lender of Last Resort: The Bank of England lending money to discount houses which otherwise have no cash to pay loans due.

Leverage: American equivalent of financial gearing. Usually calculated by taking total debt as a percentage of total assets (ie, excluding debt).

Liability: Amount due to a creditor.

Life Insurance Companies: Financial institutions which insure ('assure') lives and pay annuities, in return for premiums.

Limited Company: Now called 'public limited company' (= plc). A form of business organization with a separate legal identity, whose owners (shareholders) are not personally liable for the entity's debts.

Liquid Asset: Cash or an asset easily converted into cash (eg, debtors).

Liquid Resources: Cash or marketable securities. Would *not* normally include debtors.

Liquidation: = 'Winding-up'. The legal process of ending a company's life, by selling all its assets for cash, paying off the liabilities and distributing any residual amount to the shareholders.

Liquidation Value: The amount an asset realizes (or would realize) on liquidation, often much less than book value.

Loan Stock: Long-term loan to a company or government body, often negotiable on the Stock Exchange in the secondary market.

Long-term Liability: Liability with a maturity date more than 12 months beyond the balance sheet date.

Loss: Negative profit. Though not the aim, often the result of business.

Mainstream Corporation Tax: Main company liability to corporation tax, payable some months after the end of accounting year; reduced to the extent of ACT paid at the same time as dividends.

Market: May mean the 'capital market' for loans and equity (financial securities). More generally refers to the system of voluntary exchange of goods based on competition and private ownership of property.

Market Capitalization: Total value of securities, ie, number of shares in issue (of a company or on a whole stock exchange) multiplied by their prices in the market.

Market Risk: The non-diversifiable part of the total risk attaching to an equity investment, measured by 'beta'.

Matching the Maturity: Process of 'matching' the time-period of assets and liabilities, to reduce risk.

Maturity: Time at which a loan falls due for repayment.

Medium of Exchange: The primary function of money, to act as a means by which goods and services can be exchanged indirectly (as opposed to *direct* exchange by barter).

Merchant Bank: Accepting house. Financial institution offering banking and many advisory services to corporate and other customers.

Merger: A combination of two or more formerly independent business units into a single enterprise.

Minority Interest: Part of a group's assets *controlled* by holding company, but *owned* by 'outside' ('minority') shareholders via some of the equity shares in (one or more) subsidiary companies.

Modern Portfolio Theory (MPT): Distinguishes non-diversifiable 'market risk' and 'unique risk' which can be eliminated by holding a properly diversified portfolio. An efficient market will not compensate investors for taking (avoidable) unique risks, so the required rate of return will vary *solely* with market risk (measured by beta).

Negative Interest Rate: 'Real' interest rate, after-tax and net of inflation, which may be negative because while the inflation premium is tax-deductible the 'real' gain from inflation is not taxable.

Net Assets: = Capital employed.Fixed assets + Working capital. (= Total assets − Current liabilities.)

Net Dividend: Amount of cash dividend paid to shareholders, net of basic rate income tax (at 30 per cent of gross dividend) deducted as ACT.

Net Present Value (NPV): Discounted estimated future cash inflows minus (discounted) cash outflow(s). If positive, indicates prima facie acceptability of capital investment project.

Net Realizable Value: Net amount for which asset could be sold.

Net Terminal Value: As for NPV, but with the cash flows *compounded* to future horizon date instead of discounted back to present (value).

New Issue: First-time sale to the public of a company's securities.

Nominal Value: = 'Par value'. Face value of security, unrelated to the market value. Usually refers either to ordinary shares (eg, with nominal value of 25p each) or to government loan stocks with nominal value of £100.

Non-diversifiable Risk: Market risk.

Offer for Sale: Method of issuing shares on Stock Exchange.

Operating Lease: Lease other than financial lease, usually for short period of time, and cancellable.

Opportunity Cost: The revenue or other benefit that might have been obtained by the 'next best' alternative course of action which has been forgone in favour of the course actually taken.

Option: An agreement to buy an investment (debt, equity or commodities) at a fixed date. Traded on futures exchanges, such as the Chicago Board of Trade, London International Financial Futures Exchange (LIFFE) or many others.

Ordinary Dividend: Dividend on ordinary shares.

Ordinary Share: Share in a company representing part-ownership, and entitled to dividends if declared by directors, and to share in any residual assets remaining when company is finally wound up.

Partnership: Form of enterprise with two or more owners ('partners'), each of whom has unlimited personal liability to meet the firm's debts.

Payback: Method of evaluating capital projects which calculates how long before initial investment is 'paid back' by later cash inflows. Ignores cash inflows *after* payback, so does *not* measure 'profitability'.

Pension Fund: Financial institution ('gross fund') investing amounts set aside during working life to provide retirement pensions.

'Perfect' Capital Market: Theoretical model of a capital market with 'perfect competition', implying: no transaction costs, no taxes, no economies of scale, no institutional barriers, perfect information.

Perpetuity: Annuity payable for ever.

Placing: Method of issuing new shares on the Stock Exchange.

Portfolio: Group of different securities held by a single owner, which diversifies away some of the 'unique' risk of individual securities.

Post-project Audit: Process of monitoring capital project's outcome.

Preference Share: Form of share capital entitled to fixed rate of dividend (usually cumulative) if declared, and to repayment of a stated amount of money on winding-up, with priority over ordinary shares.

Present Value: Discounted amount of future cash receipts, equivalent to the 'value' of an asset (or security).

Price/Dividend Ratio: Share price divided by total annual dividend per share – important ratio for income-orientated investors.

Price/Earnings (P/E) **Ratio:** Market price per ordinary share divided by most recent annual earnings per share.

Price-to-Book Ratio: Share price divided by 'book value' (either shareholders' funds or net assets – both methods used).

Primary Market: Market for securities which raises new money from public.

Profit: Sales revenue less expenses, for a period.

Profit and Loss (P&L) **Account:** Accounting statement showing result (profit or loss) of operations of a business entity for a period.

Profit Margin: Operating profit as a percentage of sales revenue.

Price Turnover: Revenue less costs. Hence:

Trading Profit: Sales (usually of a division) less costs but before interest or tax.

Operating Profit: Trading profit plus property and investment profits.

Profit Before Interest and Tax (PBIT): Total operating profit of subsidiaries plus share of associated companies' profits.

Profit Before Tax (PBT or Pretax Profit): PBIT less interest payments.

Profit After Tax (PAT): PBT less actual tax payments and deferred tax.

Profit Attributable to Ordinary Shareholders: PAT less share of profit attributable to any minority shareholders in subsidiaries.

Project Finance: Method of finance whose repayments (and perhaps interest) are tied to a project's operating results.

Prospectus: Advertisement to members of public in respect of an issue of securities, subject to the rules of the Stock Exchange.

Public Sector Borrowing Requirement (PSBR): Annual amount borrowed by government to cover excess of 'public sector' spending over tax and other revenues.

Purchasing Power: Value of money. What money will buy in 'real' terms, often measured by the 'basket of goods and services' comprising the constituent items in the Retail Price Index.

Quantity Theory of Money: Theory which (oversimplified) holds that the value of money (and the rate of inflation) will in the long run be related to the amount of money issued (the 'money supply').

Quoted Security: Security traded on the Stock Exchange, with price 'quoted' daily.

Raw Materials: Input to manufacturing process, often held for a time as stock.

Receiver: Official managing company's affairs on behalf of debenture-holders or others, often as a preliminary to winding-up.

Redemption: Repayment of loan or preference capital.

Re-investment Rate: Assumption (explicit or implicit) about the rate of return able to be earned on cash inflows 're-invested' in a business during a capital project's life.

Required Rate of Return: The rate of return needed for a capital project to be profitable. Used as discount rate for NPV, as criterion for IRR.

Reserves: Shareholders' funds other than issued share capital, eg, share premium, retained profits. May not be represented by cash, so 'reserves' are *not* available for 'spending'.

Retail Price Index (RPI): Monthly statistic measuring (against base date January 1974 = 100.0) money prices of representative 'basket of goods'. The year-on-year rate of increase in the RPI is commonly regarded as 'the' annual rate of (general) inflation.

Retained Profits: Amount of profits made by a company (either for the latest year of cumulatively), and not paid out in dividends.

Return on Capital Employed (ROCE): PBT divided by capital employment.

Return on Equity: Profit after tax divided by shareholders funds.

Return on Investment (ROI): Usually means return on net assets.

Return on Net Assets: Operating profit before interest and tax (= EBIT) divided by net assets(= by capital employed) = 'Primary Efficiency Ratio'.

Return on Sales: Profit before interest and tax (PBIT or EBIT) divided by turnover (sales revenue).

Revenue: American (and increasingly, international) equivalent of turnover.

Rights Issue: Issue usually of ordinary shares, to existing shareholders to raise cash.

Risk: Volatility about a mean (average) 'expected value'. More loosely, possibility of loss (either likelihood or extent). Sometimes treated as synonymous with 'uncertainty'.

Risk Premium: Part of interest rate relating to perceived risk of investment.

Risk-free Rate of Return: Rate of return available in market on securities regarded as having *no* risk (usually only if government-guaranteed). An inflation premium is added separately.

Risk-free Securities: Government securities regarded as virtually certain to pay interest and capital amount on due dates.

Sale and Leaseback: Method of raising finance by selling capital asset for lump sum, while continuing to use it in return for lease payments. In effect, a capital disinvestment.

Secondary Market: Market for securities in which existing holders can buy and sell securities without directly involving the original issuer.

Security (collateral): Legal charge on asset(s) by lender. In the event of default, secured creditor is entitler to priority of repayment out of proceeds of disposal of the charged asset(s).

Security (share): Any stocks or shares, usually quoted.

Selling Short: Selling assets not owned, in the hope of buying back later, after the market price has fallen.

Share: Partial ownership of ordinary capital of company.

Share Premium: Excess of issue price over nominal price of share.

Share Split: Process of dividing share capital into more shares of smaller nominal amount each. Reduces market price per share pro rata without affecting the total market value.

Shareholder's Funds: Amount shown in company balance sheet as attributable to ordinary (and sometimes preference) shareholders.

Specific Risk: Unique risk of security, which can be diversified away by holding a suitable portfolio.

Speculator: Anyone who acts on view about the uncertain future.

Stag: Bull of new issues, hoping for an immediate rise in market price when dealings start, giving a quick profit on any shares alloted.

Stock (inventory): Holding of goods, either as raw materials, work in progress or finished goods, with a view to sale (perhaps after further processing) in the ordinary course of business.

Stock (share): Similar to ordinary share in company, but may be divisible into smaller money amounts for dealing purposes.

Stock Appreciation: Part of apparent HC accounting profit on stocks (inventories) due solely to an increase in their price.

Stock Exchange: Market for buying and selling securities.

Stock Relief: Tax allowance intended to prevent tax being charged on stock appreciation.

Stock Turnover: Accounting ratio dividing sales turnover for a year by amount of stock held. Reciprocal of 'days' sales in stock'.

Stockbroker: Agent for investor, on whose behalf he buys or sells shares on the Stock Exchange, dealing with jobbers (acting as principals).

Store of Wealth: Traditional function of money, impaired by inflation.

Subsidiary: Company most of whose equity shares are owned by another (its 'holding' or 'parent' company).

Synergy: What is hoped on merger to make 2 + 2 = 5. Often delusive.

Tangible Asset: Physical asset, such as property and equipment. Excludes items such as goodwill, publishing rights, route licences and brand values (intangible assets).

Tender Method: Method of issuing shares to public, leaving price to be settled by demand for shares, thus discouraging stags (who can hardly expect much further appreciation when dealing starts).

Term Loan: Loan (probably from a bank) for a fixed period of time (often between one and seven years).

Term Structure of Interest Rates: The pattern of interest rates over different periods of time, eg, from three months to 25 years.

Time Deposit: Deposit (account) with bank, withdrawable by giving a definite period of notice (often seven days), and bearing interest.

Time Preference: Ratio between someone's valuation of a good now and his valuation of an otherwise identical good at some future date.

Trade Credit: Normal business arrangement to buy and sell goods 'on credit', ie, not settling in cash until some time later.

Transaction Cost: The cost of undertaking a transaction, eg, taxes, commissions, administrative costs.

Treasury Bill: Three-month government bills of exchange.

Turn: The difference between the prices at which jobbers buy and sell securities.

Uncertainty: Lack of knowledge about the future. Differs from 'risk', which usually assumes known probabilities of possible outcomes.

Underwriter: Person or firm agreeing, for a fee, to meet the financial consequences of a risk, eg, on new share issues.

Unique Risk: Specific risk of company or project, which can be diversified away by holding a suitable portfolio (unlike market risk).

Unit of Account: Numeraire in accounting. Traditionally the monetary unit, but in times of inflation an alternative – the 'constant purchasing power unit' – has been suggested.

Unit of Constant Purchasing Power: Money amount adjusted (by reference to date of transaction) by Retail Price Index, to improve usefulness of accounting, especially in comparisons over time.

Unit Trust: Financial enterprise holding range of securities; suitable vehicle for small unit-holder to spread his risk.

Unlisted Securities Market (USM): Recently-started market for securities of companies too small for full 'listing' ('quotation'); subject to less stringent rules.

Unquoted Company: Company whose shares are not quoted on the Stock Exchange. Hence shareholders may find it hard to sell their shares.

Unrecovered ACT: ACT unable to be (fully) set off against 'mainstream' UK tax liability, eg, due to losses or profits earned abroad, which has to be written off as an extra expense.

Unsecured Creditor: Creditor without security.

Valued Added: Difference between sales revenue and cost of bought-in materials and services. Roughly = profit plus wages.

Variable Expenses: Expense which varies directly with level of output.

Venture Capital: Equity finance for high-risk new or small business.

Vertical Merger: Combination of two (or more) businesses engaged in different stages of production process in same industry, eg, brewery buying pubs, or tyre manufacturer buying rubber plantations.

Wealth: Well-offness, expressed in terms of money, normally related to (ultimately) marketable assets.

Weighted Average Cost of Capital (WACC): Average of the after-tax marginal costs of various kinds of long-term capital (debt, equity, etc), 'weighted' by their market value.

Wholesale Banking: Banking in large sums of money, with financial institutions of large companies, as opposed to 'retail' banking with members of the public.

Winding-up: = Liquidation. Process of ending a company's life, by selling all the assets, paying off creditors and distributing anything left over to ordinary shareholders.

Work-in-progress (WIP): Partly-completed stocks in manufacturing process.

Working Capital: Excess of current assets over current liabilities.

Yield: Rate of return on investment (usually security), interest or dividend divided by current market price.

Yield to Redemption: Yield on loan stock including element or capital gain anticipated when principal (nominal amount) is repaid (at 'par') on maturity, in addition to the 'flat' yield of annual interest.

Source: *Financial Decisions* by D. R. Myddleton, reproduced with the permission of the Longman Group.

Index

house brokers 7
Howell, Michael 145
Hoylake 91

IBM 144
ICI 118
image, corporate 69, 74, 159–60
Imperial Group 73, 160
Independent 12
index-linking 11, 40, 41
individual shareholders *see* private
    investors
industrial accidents 86, 95
inertia, institutional 49
information, dissemination of 13–14
Initial Public Offering (IPO) 133
Institute of Chartered Accountants of
    Scotland 71
institutional associations 105
Institutional Investor 73
institutional investors 11, 12, 13–14, 27,
    40, 42, 48–51, 98, 128, 164, 165
insurance companies 48, 49, 100, 144,
    146, 149
insurance funds 49
interim report 71–2
International Accounting Standards
    Committee (IASC) 72, 114, 115
International Brokers Estimate System
    138
International Finance Corporation 140
international IR 105–27, 175
    in Europe 144–53
    in Japan 139–43, 172
    in USA 128–38
interviews 165, 166, 167
inventories, valuing 115
investment trusts 48–9, 146
investors, defining 173
Investor Protection Committees (IPCs)
    11–12, 15, 97–8, 105–6
Investor Relations 145
investor relations, summarized 172–5
Investor Relations Guide 167
Investor Relations Society 17, 109, 118,
    148
investors *see under individual headings, eg,*
    foreign investors; institutional
    investors; private investors
IR managers 16, 19–21, 36, 56, 159, 173
    and analysts 78–9
    and chairman's statement 68–9

and debt financing 97
and importance of anticipation 62
and industrial accidents 94
and proxy votes 162
and share performance 161
and takeover bids 89, 93
qualities needed by 33–5, 173
IR role 19, 36–7, 77–8, 171, 172, 174
Ireland 146
Irving Trust 133
Italy 146, 150
Ivory and Sime 51

Jaguar 122
James Kuhn Associates 150
Japan 4, 22, 109, 113, 122, 125–6, 139–43,
    148, 170, 172
Japan Securities Clearing Corporation
    (JSCC) 141
jobbers 8, 10, 52, 134
Johnson, Johnnie D. 39
Johnson and Johnson 95
journalists 52, 53–4, 76, 165
JWT 5

Kissinger, Henry 86
knowledgeability, of IR managers 33
Korea 126, 140
Kredietbank 150
Kroll Associates 91

Lamont, Sir Norman 13
language barriers 120, 139, 151
lawyers, American 131, 133
legal costs 123, 141–2, 157–8
legal English 32
LEP Group 110, 138
'212 letters' 33, 45, 46
leveraged buy-outs 95, 108
LIFO valuation 115
listed company advisory service (LCAS)
    43
listings, overseas 105–9, 113, 114, 116,
    123–5
litigatiousness, American 131
London Business School 31
London Marathon 75
long-term shareholders 6
'long-termism' 49
Lonrho 111, 122
lunches, City 67, 78
Luxemburg 151